The Soul of the Helper Ad

"This book joins insights f.
contemplative theology, and Dr. Oxhandler's own spiritual
journey to guide helpers in transformational healing and growth.
Dr. Oxhandler's presentation of Namaste Theory nurtures
awareness of the Sacred within ourselves and those we help in a
wise, heartful, humble, and skillful way. She extends her deep
faith to embrace the diversity of everyone's spiritual paths. As a
result, her approach joins head with heart and contemplation
with active service while honoring the Sacred in all."

—**Edward R. Canda**, PhD, professor emeritus and coordinator
of the Spiritual Diversity and Social Work Initiative at
The University of Kansas, and author of *Spiritual Diversity
in Social Work Practice*

"*The Soul of the Helper* is a deep exhale and a warm embrace
for all who care for others but too easily forget to care for
themselves. Dr. Oxhandler's expansive, approachable work will
shine a guiding light into your heart, mind, body, and soul—
helping you release what is not yours to hold so that you might
be more awake to the belovedness that radiates within you and
around you."

—**Kayla Craig**, author of *To Light Their Way*

"The true gift of Dr. Oxhandler's writing is that she engages her
own curiosity and tenderly shares helpful tools to make our
inner worlds and the world around us spiritually healthier. In
this book, she helps the helpers by reminding us that our care
matters and that the world is a better place when we meet those
needs alongside recognizing the Divine in everyone. Please buy

this book and give yourself the space to read and actively embody its practices—you will be so glad you did."

—**Kaitlin Curtice**, essayist, poet, and award-winning
  author of *Native*

"In *The Soul of the Helper*, Holly Oxhandler gently reminds us that soul-work is an essential component of health, healing, and helping. A timely and much-needed read; spot on, brilliantly unpacked, and beautifully written."

—**Rev. Courtney Ellis**, PCUSA, pastor, and
  author of *Uncluttered*

"It takes a special type of person to run into the difficult situations of others. These helpers rarely see what they do as valiant or sacrificial. They are simply acting from a place of authentic desire to serve others. In *The Soul of the Helper*, Dr. Holly Oxhandler reminds them of the importance of tending to their own inner spiritual and mental landscape. Holly guides the reader through a transformational seven stage journey to seeing the Sacred, through a combination of research, personal stories, and reflection questions. *The Soul of the Helper* provides a needed framework to help those within various service professions preserve their own wellbeing as they serve others."

—**Dr. Saundra Dalton-Smith**, physician, and author of
  Sacred Rest

"Through years of academic research combined with much inner work, Dr. Holly Oxhandler offers us helpers Namaste Theory—seeing the divine spark in ourselves, and thus, in turn, being able to better observe it in others. Only in embracing our belovedness, our enoughness, God's love for us, can we identify God's image in others, their belovedness, and thus serve them well. Not only is the theory brilliant, but Oxhandler peels it back like an onion, layer by layer, teaching us how to see and embrace our belovedness. Only then can we offer others the belovedness we observe in them, back to them—the greatest of gifts! Herein we find Oxhandler an able, wise, and humble guide. It is hard to give to others what we do not have; may we learn from her how to receive it."

—**Marlena Graves**, author of *The Way Up Is Down*

"In this groundbreaking, ovarial work, Dr. Oxhandler makes ancient contemplative wisdom easily accessible and applicable to the helping professions. The field of social work and mental health will be forever enriched by Oxhandler's sound research and application of her Namaste Theory. This is a must-read not only for those in a helping career but for anyone interested in being of service to others. Thank you, Oxhandler, for living this work with your life."

—**Phileena Heuertz**, founding partner, Gravity, a Center for Contemplative Activism, and author of *Mindful Silence* and *Pilgrimage of a Soul*

"As researcher, Holly Oxhandler has shown that people want to talk about spirituality in psychotherapy and that mental health practitioners attuned to their own spirituality are more likely to attune to the spirituality of their clients. In *The Soul of the Helper*, Oxhandler becomes spiritual guide. In language rich with warmth, clarity, and humanness, she describes practical strategies to help caregivers nourish their own spiritual selves. *The Soul of the Helper* is soul food for helpers."

—**Russell Siler Jones**, ThD, LPCS, author of *Spirit in Session*, and developer of ACPE's Spiritually Integrated Psychotherapy Program

"In these days of overwhelm and trauma, *The Soul of the Helper* is a vital resource to support folks in their own healing, and ultimately in becoming a healing presence in the world. Dr. Holly Oxhandler has lovingly woven together threads of spirituality, mental health, and the inherent divine spark we each carry. I'm immensely grateful for Dr. Oxhandler's book; it's something I will return to again and again."

—**Aundi Kolber**, MA, LPC, therapist, and author of *Try Softer* and *The Try Softer Guided Journey*

"*The Soul of the Helper* is far more than a self-help book for helpers. Grounded in research yet deeply personal and profoundly practical, it's a radical invitation into greater wholeness. Whether our helping role is personal or professional, accidental or a vocational calling, this book is a guide that illuminates with clarity both the pitfalls of ignoring our limits and the promises of turning toward the Sacred within each of us."

—**Ryan Kuja**, licensed therapist, spiritual director, and author of *From the Inside Out*

"In *The Soul of the Helper*, Dr. Holly Oxhandler offers a fresh perspective on the complex intersection of spirituality and mental health, weaving in research and gently guiding readers to reflect upon their own spiritual and mental health journeys.

Written from a background in mental health and a place of humility and respect for diverse faith traditions, Holly invites fellow helpers to wake up to the divine spark within themselves and remember their identity as Beloved. This book is a vital and brilliant guide for each of us navigating the spiritual and mental health journey as we serve others."

—**Melody Moezzi**, author of *The Rumi Prescription*

"This is a book first and foremost about the spirituality of the helper. How can helpers care for others, Holly Oxhandler asks, without attending to their own souls? With wisdom, compassion, patience, and the courage to share her personal story, Oxhandler teaches helpers to see themselves and others through a sacred lens. *The Soul of the Helper* is an invaluable, indeed essential, book for helpers, regardless of their orientation to religion and spirituality, interested in weaving spirituality more fully into the ways they care for others and themselves."

—**Kenneth I. Pargament**, PhD, professor emeritus of psychology, Bowling Green State University, and author of *Spiritually Integrated Psychotherapy*

"Like many other 'helpers,' I've often been haunted by a need to work harder, do more, and serve better that's led to weariness and burnout. In *The Soul of the Helper*, Dr. Holly Oxhandler upends the lie that we can love others well if we don't truly love ourselves. With tender vulnerability and simple practices we can all implement, Dr. Oxhandler gently leads us toward a life grounded in our belovedness. If you want to love others well but want to do it from a place of rest, health, and wholeness, this poignant and timely book is for you."

—**Sarah J. Robinson**, author of *I Love Jesus, But I Want to Die*

"*The Soul of the Helper* is a timely reminder to all healthcare practitioners that taking care of others necessitates taking care of ourselves, and receiving care from others. Oxhandler masterfully interweaves her personal experiences, clinical anecdotes, and the latest research on spirituality and mental health to illustrate how a spiritual worldview can engender greater recognition of our inner greatness and that of our patients."

—**David H. Rosmarin**, PhD, assistant professor in the Department of Psychiatry at Harvard Medical School, director of the Spirituality and Mental Health Program at McLean Hospital, and author of *The Connections Paradigm*

"It's truly the vulnerability for me. Dr. Oxhandler's truth in the words of *The Soul of the Helper* is inspiring and breathtaking. It reads as if I'm having my own personal conversation with her in my living room. The reflection exercises are profound and yet still easily applicable to the everyday experience of a helper. One will truly connect or re-connect with the Sacred within them after reading this book."

—**Dr. Amber Thornton**, clinical psychologist, and motherhood wellness consultant

"Well-researched and incredibly written, *The Soul of The Helper* is an outstanding resource. Dr. Oxhandler blends her own story with practical ideas that are important for anyone that calls themselves a helper, regardless of the context."

—**Robert Vore**, therapist, and host of *CXMH: A Podcast on Faith & Mental Heath*

THE SOUL OF THE HELPER

THE
SOUL
OF THE
HELPER

Seven Stages to Seeing
the Sacred Within Yourself
So You Can See It in Others

HOLLY K. OXHANDLER, PHD, LMSW

TEMPLETON PRESS

Templeton Press
300 Conshohocken State Road, Suite 500
West Conshohocken, PA 19428
www.templetonpress.org

First paperback edition, 2025
ISBN 978-1-59947-110-5

Set in Minion Pro and Proxima Nova by Westchester Publishing Services.

This paper meets the requirements of ANSI/NISO Z39.48-1992
(Permanence of Paper).

ISBN: 978-1-59947-591-2 (cloth)
ISBN: 978-1-59947-592-9 (ebook)

Library of Congress Control Number: 2021945297

A catalogue record for this book is available from the Library of Congress.

Printed in the United States of America.

Distributed worldwide by Rutgers University Press

To Callie and Oliver

May you always seek the light within you throughout your journey, which I'm so grateful and honored to get to walk alongside. Thank you for teaching me to be present, to heal, and to play.

To Cory

May you always know how much you mean to me and how grateful I am for you. Thank you for teaching me to slow down, for loving me as I am, and for always believing in me.

CONTENTS

PART I Spirituality and Mental Health: Two Key Considerations for Seeking the Sacred Within

PART II The Journey of Seeking the Sacred: Finding the Sacred Within Ourselves to See It in Others

PART III **"So What?": Cultivating a Practice of Seeking and Serving the Sacred for the Journey Ahead**

AUTHOR'S NOTE

This book includes content on the intersection of spirituality and mental health. It is written from the perspective of a social work researcher who studies and has personally navigated this intersection. It is also generally written using a qualitative research method called autoethnography. This approach involves being reflexive and weaving in elements of my personal story alongside the research to better understand the data and experiences of someone navigating this intersection.

More specifically, I consider myself to be a helper, particularly as a parent, partner, educator, researcher, social worker, administrator, loved one, and fellow human being who deeply values and finds meaning in serving others. My graduate training in social work focused on mental health, and I have personally navigated anxiety and depression. My faith background is in Catholicism and Protestant Christianity, with some interfaith experiences described in the book. To be clear, I am not writing this book as a religious scholar or faith leader. Any mention of other religious traditions, cultures, or philosophies are to the best of my understanding and with a wholehearted posture of humility and respect. While elements of my mental health and spiritual journey may resonate with you as a fellow traveler, it is simply *one* journey and I encourage you to lean into your own unique spiritual and mental health journey.

Throughout this book, you'll find resources that might help you navigate your own mental health and spiritual journey. As a fellow traveler who has navigated this complex intersection in my own life, let me assure you—books can be helpful along the journey but cannot replace the hard work of seeing a trained mental health care provider or spiritual director (or both).

If you or someone you love is facing mental health or spiritual struggles, help is available. You are so worth caring for and tending to the gift of your life, and my wholehearted hope is that after reading this book, you will see and know it for yourself.

INTENTION

Dear fellow helper,

I have a hunch that along your journey you've been taught to help others and to do and go and alleviate and advocate and heal and serve. If you're reading this book, you likely consider yourself a helper in some capacity. Maybe you're a parent, therapist, teacher, barista, doctor, or faith leader. Maybe you're a social worker, lawyer, caregiver, community volunteer, or public servant. No matter your role, you are a complex being. You have physical, social, mental, emotional, and spiritual needs, all of which are worth tending to the best of your ability.

In this book, I'll be asking you to consider the roles of faith and mental health in your own life. I promise to explain this more in the chapters ahead and why this is so important, but for now, know this: I'm writing this book with you in my mind, heart, and being. I'm picturing you, imagining your face, the way you smile, and the way you share your gifts with your community. I imagine your heart's heaviness from practicing empathy each day, your incredible resilience, and the unique and complex faith and mental health journeys you navigate, even as you serve the world around you.

The way you care for others is holy, sacred work. You bring healing to so many in the good work you do. Regardless of whether you see it, you are birthing beauty, love, goodness, and wholeness into the world. As a fellow human being, parent, teacher, loved one, and helper—thank you.

In the pages ahead, I hope to honor you and the ways you care for others. At the same time, know that I deeply care for you just as you are, aside from anything you do. Why? Because you bear the image of divinity. You are beloved exactly as you are, and that alone makes you worthy of honor and dignity.

That's why I intend to serve you in this book with the hope that in the pages ahead you will not only see the image of God in yourself, but you will see it in those you serve. Even more, it's my hope that you will learn to better serve the Sacred in yourself and others, nurturing the divine spark that is in you.

Kindly,

holly

THE SOUL OF THE HELPER

INTRODUCTION

I don't belong here, I thought, as the resident students in their white coats filled up the front seats of the auditorium. Pairs of middle-aged men—psychiatrists, psychologists, and physicians—engaged in small talk in the aisles. I couldn't hear their conversations, but I assumed they were discussing topics well beyond my comprehension. I hid in a back corner, rows away from anyone. I was only twenty-three and months away from beginning a master's degree in social work. I was out of my league.

Dr. Kenneth Pargament, a psychology professor and well-known researcher on religious coping, was visiting the Texas Medical Center to give a presentation entitled *God Help Me: Addressing Religious Resources and Spiritual Struggles in the Context of Health Care.* At the time, I was working as a research assistant on a study examining how older adults in therapy for anxiety and depression viewed the role of religion or spirituality in their treatment. Having heard these patients' stories and navigated my own life circumstances through both faith and therapy, I suspected Dr. Pargament's work would resonate.

He began by presenting data on how patients use faith to cope with difficulties. Through his research, he demonstrated how religion and spirituality were inextricably tied to mental health.[1] And then he shared a startling statistic I've never forgotten: nearly 90 percent of U.S. adults believe in God, but about a third of psychologists believe in a personal God, and very few psychology programs include attention to the role of religion or spirituality in practice.[2]

But these are helpers, people trained to serve others, I thought. And with so many who believe in God and use that belief to cope with the stresses of life, shouldn't these therapists be trained to help their clients bridge the gap between their mental health and their faith?

Sitting in the back corner of the auditorium, my stomach, heart, and jaw all dropped at the same time. Every cell in my body hummed with curiosity. As I scribbled some notes, my thoughts shifted to the profession I'd soon be studying. Without thinking, I wrote, *What about social work?*, wondering if the same gap existed in that field. Were social workers trained to consider the spiritual beliefs and needs of those they helped? I circled the question over and over in a state of meditation, surrender, and deep curiosity. Time stood still, and it was as though gravity was anchoring me to that question.

Over the months that followed, that question that hit me like a lightning bolt—*What about social work?*—kept nagging at me. It wouldn't let me go. It never has. That question and my deep curiosity surrounding it set the stage for what has become my life's work.

More specifically, for the last thirteen years, I've contemplated how mental health professionals can ethically and effectively integrate clients' religion and spirituality into treatments meant to help people. I've read the work of other scholars asking similar questions in social work and related disciplines. I've developed my own research studies on the topic, gathered the data, and written about my findings in peer-reviewed academic journals.[3] In doing so, I've realized this isn't just a question for mental health care providers or social workers to consider but for everyday helpers. That's what I want to share with you in this book. But first, you might be wondering how I ended up in that auditorium in the first place. It's a great question, one that begins in my childhood.

Early Seeds: My Journey into the Soul of a Helper

I was only ten when my parents began a long, messy divorce that included a painfully complex custody battle. Even after being finalized, years of residual heartache and trauma continued. Through all of it, I navigated a turbulent relationship with my biological father that included moments of joy but also fear, abuse, and rejection. Fortunately, even in the 1990s, my mother understood the importance of therapy during this season of transition, trauma, and grief.

Throughout those years, many therapists heard my story— Rosie, Peter, Estalyn, Alexia, Angela—and I'm grateful for the safety and care each provided. In their offices, I felt safe to set down my mask, quit pretending I was "okay" to comfort others, and invite them into my heavy interior world.

Growing up Catholic, faith was always important to me. I attended Catholic schools, went to church every Sunday, and participated in or received the age-appropriate sacraments. But faithful as I appeared, I was also wrestling with and deconstructing my faith, even at a young age. None of my friends had divorced parents, and I didn't talk about my home situation because our school and church didn't make space for divorce. For example, one day in fourth grade, with my overnight bag tucked in the classroom corner because of my parents' joint-custody schedule, my religion teacher shared her understanding of the Church's position on divorce with the class. "If you get a divorce, you're going to hell," she said, and all eyes turned to me. As the swell of shame and confusion set in, I ran across the room, curled up against the doorframe, and cried hot tears. It was the beginning of my long process of questioning my faith. Even more, it was the first time I sensed that not all helpers—which includes teachers—are always helpful.

When combined with the shame I felt at school, the trauma and abuse I experienced from my biological father complicated my relationship with God. I lived in constant fear that I'd disappointed God by breaking the fifth commandment: "Honour thy father and thy mother" (Exodus 20:12, KJV). After all, how could I honor my biological father who was actively hurting me? And why would God allow this kind of abuse and rejection to happen in my life? Struggling through these questions, I wondered, *Am I enough as I am for God's love?*

I went to confession seeking forgiveness, but I struggled to connect with a heavenly Father because my relationship with my biological father was so fractured. More than one priest was speechless as I shared about my home life, sobbing in fear that God would reject me just like my father had. And oh, how my father had rejected me. In one court-filed custody document, he'd described our relationship as meaningless.

But where my priests were speechless, my childhood therapists offered hope and healing. They were comfortable asking about my shame, anxiety, and grief. Some asked about my faith and infused it into treatment. For example, Peter spoke with me about meaning, purpose, God, and the role of faith in navigating my suffering—not to bypass my suffering but to hold space for all I was carrying. He had Indigenous imagery and sacred objects throughout his office, which opened my heart to a more expansive spirituality, and I later discovered he was a student of Fr. Richard Rohr's Living School.[4] Another therapist had Buddhist and Hindu symbols around her office, further exposing me to the mystery of diverse world religions as I sought support, and like Peter, she helped me connect with my faith on the journey toward healing. And as my interests in the intersection of faith and mental health grew during college, yet another therapist shared stories of liminal spaces and sacred moments when time stood still with her clients.[5]

While some of my therapists were comfortable discussing spirituality, others were not. When I shared the importance of my faith, one replied, "Um, hmm, okay . . . but we won't be talking about *that* in here." Prickles of shame crept up, and in later sessions I always hesitated before mentioning my faith.

Years later, as I consider what my academic research has taught me, I'm not surprised by my therapists' varying degrees of comfort. Peter was by far the most comfortable and curious. He never pushed a religious belief or agenda. Instead, he remained deeply grounded in what he believed, which allowed me the space I needed to explore my own faith, particularly as it related to my mental health and family situations. I wholly trusted Peter's groundedness. In fact, it informs my work today.

I wish we each had someone like Peter in our lives, but more importantly, I wish we could be like Peter for others, even if we're not all therapists. Why? Because we cannot separate our mental health from our spiritual journeys.

Early Seeds: My Journey into the Social Work Profession

My experiences as a child led me to want to care for others. So, after receiving my bachelor's degree in psychology, I was connected with a research team at Baylor College of Medicine that was studying a therapy manual for older adults with anxiety and depression.[6]

For a year, I offered eight-week sessions to these older adults and was trained in cognitive behavioral therapy. I also had an opportunity to work on the team's adjacent research study, interviewing older adults regarding if they wanted to discuss their religion and spirituality in mental health treatment. I fell in love with this second study. As one who'd had such mixed experiences with the confluence of faith and therapy, I was curious how older and wiser patients might navigate it.

Over the course of that study, we found that four out of five older adults wanted to discuss faith as it related to their mental health.[7] Over half said a therapist should bring up religion and spirituality during therapy, while a slim 17 percent said the client should bring the topic up. (Others said either could bring it up.) Why did most older adults want to include their faith within their mental health treatment? More, why had I heard "we don't talk about spirituality" in some of my training and from my own therapist?

I hadn't answered these questions when I left the team in 2009 to begin my master's degree in social work at the University of Houston, and they kept nagging at me. As my new colleagues and I sat in that auditorium those first few days, the faculty presented basic social work content to orient us. We were taught to think about our future clients holistically, as biopsychosocial individuals whose physical health, mental health, and social support are interconnected. We learned the phrase "person-in-environment," which captures how our environment and surrounding people, policies, structures, and systems influence us. We discussed ethics, coping, communities, resilience, trauma, and diverse layers of intersectionality.

What was the one thing we really didn't hear about during orientation? The role of religion, spirituality, or faith in social work. It was curious, especially because each presented topic was connected to religion and spirituality. It was also unsettling after working on the study a few months prior and hearing how many older adults wanted to talk about their spirituality in treatment, preferring that the therapist bring it up. With social work providing the largest proportion of mental health care in the United States, wouldn't these topics matter in our profession?[8]

As the semester continued, I pressed into my curiosity and found few researchers were studying spirituality and social work, leaving many gaps in understanding. In fact, across mental health fields, researchers studying this topic were few and far between. And though I began my master's training with the intention of having a private practice, I kept returning to Dr. Pargament's lecture and that question I scribbled down. I considered the studies I was reading that pointed to a lack of training on spirituality in social work and related professions. So, midway into my graduate training, I charted a new path toward a PhD, studying the integration of spirituality in social work practice.[9] I knew it was the right move. I'd fallen in love with a topic I couldn't *not* study.

The Why Behind This Book

After studying the connection between faith and mental health for over a decade, this research has humbled and transformed me. It's taught me an important lesson: we all hold sacred beliefs and lived experiences, and those beliefs and experiences are important to consider in mental health care treatment. In fact, those beliefs and experiences are important to consider in any work of service. What's more, if we—the helpers—aren't paying attention to our own spiritual and mental health journeys, we run the risk of unintentionally hurting those we're trying to care for. It may lead us to say things like what one of my therapists said to me—we won't be talking about that (i.e., spirituality) here.

As I'll explain in this book, our work as helpers is most grounded when we see and serve the Sacred within both ourselves and those we're helping. The concept of seeing the Sacred in ourselves and others can be captured in a Sanskrit word, *Namaste,* which comes from the words *namah* meaning "to bow or bend" and *te* meaning "to you."[10] *Namaste* is commonly translated as "the Sacred in me honors the Sacred in you," or "the God in me recognizes the God in you," and it is often spoken as a greeting with folded hands and a bow.[11]

In 2017, I developed a grounded theory based on this research with mental health care providers that I called Namaste Theory.[12] As I've thought more about this theory, contemplated it within my own life, and been in conversation with other helpers, I've realized it's a theory meant to help "helpers"—anyone who cares for another human being—recognize the Sacred within themselves. Why? Because my research showed that when helpers see and serve the Sacred within themselves, they are more likely to see and serve the Sacred within those they care for.

Transparently, I worked for years without seeing and serving the Sacred in myself. I had bought the lie that even if I wasn't caring for myself holistically, I was still capable of caring for others (hello, pride). I thought I could push past my own exhaustion and continue helping. But as you'll see, this was not the case. The fact is, when our well becomes empty, we fall into exhaustion, resentment, and burnout in our efforts to help others. As helpers, we need to find a way to keep our wells full.

An Overview of the Book

Parents, partners, friends, colleagues, therapists, teachers, faith leaders, spiritual directors, administrators, leaders, engineers, waiters, medical doctors, nurses, office managers, social workers, politicians, authors, researchers, baristas, retail employees, first responders, artists, performers, custodial staff, lawyers, caregivers—nearly everyone has the capacity to be a helper. But some of the most helpful helpers operate from a place of holistic health, including humbly integrating spirituality with their mental health journey. What's more, they recognize spirituality can be a central element to their lives and the lives of others. In the pages ahead, I'll share how Namaste Theory—recognizing the Sacred within ourselves and others—can help you live into that kind of framework.

In Part I, I'll demonstrate the importance of viewing mental health on a spectrum. I'll discuss the complexity of religion and spirituality and their connection with mental health. Then I'll introduce Namaste Theory and the research behind it, and conclude with a call for helpers to practice self-awareness as we serve.

Part II will cover the journey of seeking the Sacred, first within yourself, then in others. Each chapter—Speed, Slow, Steady, Still, See, Shift, Serve—outlines a step we must take on our journey toward seeing the Sacred in ourselves and others. Each chapter also includes relevant practices to help us connect with and serve the Sacred within the core of our being and within those around us.

The book concludes with the question I ask at the end of every class: "So what?" Considering Namaste Theory and this seven-stage journey, I'll invite you to reflect on why it matters to you and how it relates to the ways you support others.

My wholehearted hope is that these chapters help you reawaken to your inherent worth and help you see the Sacred within yourself, and that by doing so, you'll see it in others. I hope you'll trust me as a humble guide—not as someone who has perfected this process but as a fellow traveler on this lifelong journey of seeking the Sacred.

PART I

Spirituality and Mental Health

Two Key Considerations for Seeking the Sacred Within

CHAPTER 1

Considering the Spiritual Journey

*Faith does not need to push the river precisely
because it is able to trust that there is a river.
The river is flowing; we are in it.*[1]

—Fr. Richard Rohr

"Just pick a box!"

A dear colleague looks at me in a virtual meeting as I try to find an answer that best fits the question, "What's your religious affiliation?" My answer—Catholic, Protestant, Buddhist, None, whatever—will help a part of the work we're doing, and I think he'd like to hurry me along. But if I'm honest, I don't think my spiritual journey neatly fits within any of these boxes. How can a lifetime of dynamic beliefs, experiences, practices, and even doubts fit within a tiny square?

Struggling to answer, my mind wanders to one of the richest conversations I've had on spirituality with a prominent social work scholar. As we walked together outside a conference hall in 2013, she asked about my dissertation research. I sensed her cautious curiosity as I explained that I was studying social workers' attention to clients' spirituality in treatment. As we walked under the old trees on campus, she disclosed that she identified as atheist and shifted into a beautifully poetic explanation of her preference for the words *wonder*, *awe*, and *beauty*.

Listening to this academic draw on examples of what these words meant, I watched with deep curiosity as something tangibly shifted in her. Her whole being softened while simultaneously lighting up, and her voice became tender. For this academic, these terms—wonder, awe, beauty, mystery, presence—touched on something sacred within her and her connection with everything, which couldn't be ignored, corrected, or dismissed. And in that moment, I recognized the honor of holding vulnerable space to listen to what these words meant to this fellow image-bearer of God who didn't believe in God.

I return to the boxes, continue to contemplate them. There's no option for "Wonder." There's no option for "Awe" or "Mystery" or even "Spiritual." Instead, every option is hard and fast. I am either one religious tradition or another, and the rules don't allow me to check more than one box or add caveats to the side. It is an impossible task, so I simply choose "Protestant" and move on.

Religion and Spirituality

The Latin root of spirituality, *spiritus*, means "breath of life," and I've loved Dr. Pargament's simple definition of spirituality over the years: "the search for the sacred."[2] For the purpose of this book, I want to stretch this definition a bit further and define spirituality as follows: *The experiential search of the mystical, sacred spark or image of God within that connects us to our truest selves, to one another, and to all that surrounds us.* Spirituality, in other words, cultivates an inner sense of connection with the immanent and transcendent sacred love found in others and in all of creation.

My reference to the image of God within us is from Genesis 1:26–27 and reflects this idea of the sacred spark, which has been written across various mystical traditions. As Christian mystic

Meister Eckhart notes, there is a "light in the soul that is uncreated and uncreatable," an essence within the soul that cannot be separated from God. Eckhart explains that our purpose in life is to discover this divine spark in our own hearts and then realize this spark is in all of life.[3]

Religion is quite different, although it has some overlap with spirituality when it comes to our emotions, thoughts, and experiences. As noted by social work professor and researcher Dr. Edward Canda, religion is a "systematic pattern of values, beliefs, symbols, behaviors, and experiences that are oriented toward spiritual concerns shared by a community and transmitted over time in traditions."[4]

For many of us, our spirituality brings us together and leads us to organize within certain religions. These religions attempt to guide us in our spiritual interactions. Put another way, spirituality is generally (and hopefully) the focus of religion, though that isn't always the case.

Another relevant term you'll see threaded in this book is *faith*. Professor and theologian Dr. James Fowler defines faith as "a generic feature of the human struggle to find and maintain meaning [that] may or may not find religious expression."[5] For many of us though, our faith is inherently connected to both religion and spirituality.

Just as we are biological, psychological, and social beings, we are also spiritual beings. As a result, similar to how we experience physical health, psychological health, and social health (relationships with friends, loved ones, and others) on a spectrum, we also experience spirituality on a spectrum of "health." Like these other areas of our lives, spirituality can be neglected or cultivated, starved or strengthened, or change in ways beyond our control. Spirituality develops over time, not in a prescriptive, linear fashion but through complex and layered growth based on experiences, supports, resources, and needs.

Religious Affiliation, Beliefs, and Practices

As of 2015, three out of four adults in the United States consider religion to be important in their lives, with 71 percent identifying with a Christian tradition, 2 percent Jewish, and about 1 percent Muslim, 1 percent Buddhist, 1 percent Hindu, or 1 percent Other.[6] About one in four are unaffiliated or not religious at all. Even within these categories, there are additional subgroups and blended belief systems.

These percentages and ways of organizing information help us generally understand where we are grouped in terms of our religious affiliation, but they do not capture the nuances within each group's or individual's experiences, views, beliefs, and practices. One person may identify as Protestant and fiercely advocate for the recognition of same-sex marriage, while another Protestant might fiercely fight against the recognition of same-sex marriage. Both might cite their faith as the motivation for their advocacy. Meanwhile, a Catholic and a Buddhist may find more in common in their daily meditation practice than a Catholic and a Protestant, though the Catholic and Protestant both identify as Christian. Similarly, a Jewish rabbi and a Muslim imam may connect over discussions of mystical experiences and find authors from the other's religious tradition who help them grow closer to God in their own journey.

Put another way, just because two individuals identify with the same religious tradition doesn't mean their beliefs, practices, and interpretations of holy texts are the same. Likewise, just because two individuals identify with different religious traditions does not mean their spiritual beliefs and practices don't align, at least in some ways. We are complex beings, each on our own journey.

In addition, spirituality and religion can have a degree of fluidity and change as we age. In fact, nearly half of us don't identify with the religious tradition of our youth.[7] And this doesn't take into account those who have left and returned to the tradition of their youth or those who are currently deconstructing and reconstructing their faith, even though they haven't yet jumped ship. I've experienced this firsthand. I grew up within the Catholic church, and my husband, Cory, grew up within the Church of Christ. Grateful as we are for the spiritual lessons we learned in our upbringing, over the course of our marriage we've attended nondenominational, Nazarene, and Baptist churches. For us, the priority has always been connecting with fellow travelers within a local faith community that closely aligns with our values and honors where we currently are as a family along our faith journey.

These days, we hear a lot about religious affiliation numbers and the decline or growth of various denominations. And though those numbers might offer a snapshot of trends and how many members there are in each group, they can be reductionistic or overly simplistic. The data points fail to capture the depth, complexity, and nuance of each respondent's spiritual journey.

In 2018, the General Social Survey reported that 78 percent of U.S. adults consider themselves to be religious and 89 percent identify as spiritual.[8] A few years prior, the Pew Research Center reported that nine in ten believe in a higher power or God, and seven in ten believe in heaven.[9] Roughly half of us feel a sense of spiritual well-being and wonder weekly.[10] These and other data points indicate that although the U.S. population is still largely religious, there seems to be a shift toward spirituality. People may attend religious services less, but at least half of adults in the United States practice their faith by praying daily, a third read scripture weekly, and 40 percent meditate at least weekly.[11] Even among those who consider themselves unaffiliated, atheist, or agnostic, three out of five believe in God, two out of five feel spiritual peace and well-being weekly, and one in five pray daily.[12]

These private and communal religious or spiritual practices are important to consider as we think about how we and those we care for lean on faith in times of joy and struggle.

The Spiritual Journey

Some philosophers, psychologists, and spiritual teachers have written about various stages of faith or spiritual movements in an effort to help us understand the complexity of our spiritual growth and development. Examples of these include Dr. James Fowler's *Stages of Faith*, Ken Wilber's *Integral Theory*, Dr. Abraham Maslow's *Hierarchy of Needs* (which later included self-transcendence), and Phileena Heuertz's *Pilgrimage of a Soul*, among others.[13] Each of these offers a robust examination of the shape of the spiritual life, which grows and develops like our bodies and minds. Each highlights the fact that the spiritual life requires care, attention, and practice, and sometimes progress is slow.

In his work, Dr. Fowler notes there are seven stages of faith, in which a person moves from the "infancy and undifferentiated" stage to the "universalizing faith" stage.[14] Although aging plays an important role in biological and intellectual development, Fowler notes that progression through stages of faith doesn't happen automatically as we age. What's more, the speed of navigating through each stage can vary, and people may remain in any stage for most if not all of their adult lives.

Spiritual director and teacher Phileena Heuertz makes a similar observation in her book *Pilgrimage of a Soul*. She highlights seven nonlinear stages of spirituality—awakening, longing, darkness, death, transformation, intimacy, and union—and notes:

Picture seven three-dimensional rings all interlocked. Each ring represents a movement or season in the soul's development. During a process of formation, the soul moves throughout these rings at various times, in no particular order. The spiritual journey is more cyclical than linear. Each moment in a certain movement or ring provides a necessary experience for personal and spiritual growth and development. At times we may progress from one ring to another, only to find ourselves revisiting a former ring for a deeper work in our ever-expanding soul.[15]

Recognizing that this is a lifelong process, Heuertz explains, "We continue in this cyclical pilgrimage until that final day when we will make our last passage from death to life and find ourselves in eternal, constant union with the One whom we have longed for since we took our first breath."[16]

This spiritual journey requires time, patience, and a degree of commitment to the process. Just as the frontal lobe in our brain doesn't fully develop until around age twenty-five, and our hair doesn't naturally gray until later in life, it also takes time for our spiritual growth and development to unfold.

This ongoing journey might help us understand why it can be more difficult to make space for spiritual perspectives outside of our own when we are young or earlier along in our stages of faith. But the more grounded we are in our journey, the more we can curiously seek to understand others' perspectives, the more empathetic we can be with those around us, including those we serve. It allows us to find how and where connections lie between our journey and another's journey.

Speaking of the spiritual journey, a mentor of mine, historian and gerontologist Dr. Andy Achenbaum, offered the analogy of a tapestry or painting. The closer we stand to the image, he said, the more details and colors we see, even though we cannot see the whole picture. The farther we step back, the more of the image we can see, even though we can still pick out the spot that once held our attention. Similarly, the closer we stand to our early perspectives along the spiritual journey, the less we're able to humbly hold space to see and have empathy for another's journey or even our own evolving journey. Or put another way, if we refuse to take a step back, we miss out on other perspectives and experiences that can help us to see a bigger picture along our unique spiritual journey.

As helpers, we need to humbly take a few steps back and recognize that we are all on a spiritual journey, each of us viewing life from a different angle. We may have an inch of the big picture we're most familiar with, but others may be most familiar with another inch. Our invitation is to be grounded within our own individual understanding, while humbly and curiously acknowledging the experience of the other. And as helpers, we may also be invited to help others step back and see the picture too, reminding fellow travelers that we are on a spiritual journey together.

As we'll see in the next chapter, what is true for the spiritual journey is true for the mental health journey. After all, our spirituality is inextricably connected with our mental health, and so, it's important that our journeys toward mental health and spiritual development be considered in tandem.

Reflection Exercises

Reflect upon what the terms religion and spirituality mean to you. Are you spiritual but not religious? Religious but not spiritual? Neither? Both? Has your understanding of what these terms mean changed over the course of your life?

How have your religious or spiritual beliefs changed over the years? What has helped shape those beliefs, including relationships, experiences, and understandings? Journal your thoughts.

Can you think of a time when someone you were helping was focused on one part of the bigger picture, especially related to their faith? Can you think of a time in which you struggled to help them and why it was difficult?

CHAPTER 2

Considering the Mental Health Journey

Owning our story can be hard but not nearly as difficult as spending our lives running from it. Embracing our vulnerabilities is risky but not nearly as dangerous as giving up on love and belonging and joy—the experiences that make us the most vulnerable. Only when we are brave enough to explore the darkness will we discover the infinite power of our light.[1]

—Dr. Brené Brown

Shortly after moving to Waco in June 2014, I scheduled some teletherapy sessions with a licensed therapist who knew of my childhood experiences. I was overwhelmed with all of our family's transition—a new city, new jobs, new colleagues at a new university. There was new loneliness from being three hours away from our loved ones and new stress from not having nearby family to help with our daughter. Only months into the move, and I was struggling with the adjustment. What's more, a handful of personal and family issues were simultaneously occurring. I was doing my best to cope, but still, I began noticing some unhealthy thought patterns and coping mechanisms surfacing.

Mental health professionals use unhealthy coping mechanisms, too?

You bet.

When the stress kicked in, I filled up on chocolate. I began skipping meals and traded hours of sleep for excessive work, often grinding out twelve-hour days, six days a week. I started most days with two or three cups of coffee and ended them with one or two glasses of wine because, *hey, I'd had a long and hard day.*

The handful of teletherapy sessions helped, but deep down, I knew I needed to do this healing work in a local therapist's office. I needed a trained provider to pick up on my mannerisms and body language, someone who could compare what I said against what my body was saying. Still, I didn't make it a priority, in part because I was afraid of not finding the right therapist and in part because Waco is such a small town. Even being in this line of work and advocating for others to go to therapy, I was petrified about what others would think if they knew my story.

Of course, life has a funny way of showing us what we need when we least expect it. In 2016, our five-family church group went through a Twelve Step recovery curriculum together in preparation for the new recovery ministry our church was launching. Expert in human behavior as I was, I offered to serve this ministry after its launch. And as I delved into the material and encountered the Twelve Steps, I was humbled.[2] It helped me realize there was a great deal of buried pain in my own life, and I was numbing that pain with my unhealthy coping mechanisms instead of moving toward and through the process of healing it.

I began working the Steps, but it'd take a year to admit I needed to go even further. I needed one-on-one work with a therapist, someone who could help me get to the root of my unhealthy coping mechanisms. Someone who could push me to answer the simplest question honestly—*Why had I become a people-pleasing workaholic who was repeatedly burning out in my efforts to help others?* Like ripping a Band-Aid off, I mustered up the courage to call a local therapist, and by some miracle, he was able to get me in that afternoon.

Nearly every week for the past four years, I've visited his office and peeled back the layers of wounding—some from childhood, some from adulthood. He's helped me unlearn the white-knuckling, people-pleasing, achievement-based strategies I've used to navigate this life, and he's helped me learn to be kind to myself. His office is the safe space I offer myself each week, the place I set everything down, name the emotions deep within, and discern what I need to heal. I unpack my life, inspect my areas of unhealth, contemplate healthier ways of living, and continue on to the week as best as I can with his tender support. (Thank you, Rod.) And I know many of you are doing something similar.

As a social worker, the privilege to see a therapist each week is not lost on me. At the same time, I know this part of my mental health journey is important for me, my loved ones, and those I serve. The same is true for you.

Mental Health Problems—Everyone's Got 'Em

At some point in our lives, over 80 percent of us will meet the criteria for a diagnosable mental health struggle.[3] Should this come as any surprise? The brain is living, human, imperfect, and has the potential for sickness just like any other organ in our body. This is particularly true if we don't provide it with proper nutrition, rest, and exercise, or if we're surrounded by an unhealthy environment within our work, home, or community. And when you couple a lack of care or a toxic environment with life events beyond our control—the company layoffs that cost you your job, your parents' divorce, the onset of a global pandemic—it's a wonder that any of us think we are getting out of this life without a mental health struggle at *some* point.

Of course, some of us will struggle more with mental health issues than others. In fact, one out of five of us are currently struggling with a mental health condition.[4] Some of us need daily medication to regulate our body's chemistry. Some of us need a sponsor or accountability partner, Twelve Step meetings, or routine therapy appointments to keep us from falling back into addiction. Some will face night terrors, experience panic during typically normal activities because of past trauma, or require a contingency plan for unexpected anxiety triggers. Some have seen the inside of an emergency room or psychiatric unit.

For the record, mental health struggles don't make you weak or weird. They make you human. I've struggled with depression and anxiety off and on throughout my life. Some of these struggles are due to my childhood trauma and abuse. Some are due to my family history, which is checkered with mental health struggles and addiction. To some degree, I've fought the symptoms of depression and anxiety daily for years, some days seeming better than others. And yes, there were times when I needed medication to ensure my brain had enough dopamine to lift the cloud of despair, to get out of bed and care for myself, and to have enough energy to function through the day. And though I haven't needed those medications in a while, I am grateful to know that treatment is available if I ever need it again.

There was nothing I did to cause the trauma I experienced, and I did not choose depression and anxiety as my lot in life. These consequences of being human have simply been part of my reality, and both my faith and my mental health treatment have helped me to cope. And just as we wouldn't tell someone with diabetes to pray away their diabetes, we should *never* tell someone with clinically diagnosed mental illness that increased spiritual practices alone will cure what ails them. Rather, we should refer them to trained therapists or psychiatrists who can help them on their mental health journeys. We should affirm simple medical truths: we can have faith *and* take antidepressants; we can pray *and* see a therapist; we can worship God *and* feel the weight of mental illness.

Considering the Mental Health Journey and Spiritual Journey Together

Many of us have personally faced mental health diagnoses and treatment, but *all* of us have walked alongside a loved one experiencing a mental health challenge. If you or your friend find yourself in this situation, the answer is not to just pray more or read your sacred text more or visit your house of worship more frequently. These may help to some degree, but prioritizing your mental health might require a trip to a licensed therapist or medical doctor.

As Franciscan teacher Richard Rohr notes, *"If we do not transform our pain, we will most assuredly transmit it*—usually to those closest to us: our family, our neighbors, our co-workers, and, invariably, the most vulnerable, our children."[5] So, if you're currently doing the work to move toward emotional and mental healing, *thank you.* If you are courageously taking medication (and battling the side effects), seeing a therapist, participating in cognitive behavioral therapy (CBT) or EMDR or ACT or DBT, attending recovery meetings, or seeking any other kind of mental health treatment, you're on the right path.[6] You are taking your mental health journey seriously and breaking the cycle of pain so you do not transmit it to those around you. By facing and healing your pain, you are helping to heal this world.

And if you are a parent or caregiver, I hope you will consider normalizing going to therapy for your children, especially since half of all cases of mental illness begin by age fourteen and 75 percent by age twenty-four.[7] In light of my professional training and my experience with therapy as a child, I often wonder what would happen if we considered mental health treatment like physical health treatment. What if we treated mental health care as involving both preventative efforts (such as annual or biannual checkups) and symptom management or long-term care?

As you tend to your mental health journey, consider your spiritual journey. In recent years, there has been an increase in research looking at the ways religion and spirituality are tied to mental health, both positively and negatively. What does this mean? As we'll see below, it means it's worth considering the two in tandem.

As the medical model became the standard of care in the early 1900s, psychological treatments relied more and more on quantifiable research. And given that there was little research to support the consideration of religion or spirituality in mental health treatment throughout most of the twentieth century, psychology and related professions often dismissed the role of faith in patients' lives. In addition, because few mental health care providers considered themselves religious, and some vocal scholars (like Sigmund Freud) were opposed to religion, it isn't surprising that a patient's spirituality was often removed from their psychological treatment.[8]

Over the last few decades, however, more researchers have studied the role of religion and spirituality in mental health care.[9] What does their research teach us about the relationship between these areas of our lives and how it relates to everyday helpers? Simply put, our religion and spirituality are important when it comes to our mental health. In fact, when a client's religion or spirituality (whatever the client may believe) is ethically and effectively considered within mental health treatment, guess what happens?[10] Treatment is either as effective as traditional care or more effective— *they get better, faster.*[11]

Historically, most studies focused on the association of two or more variables (e.g., the relationship between anxiety symptoms and religious service attendance frequency) to better understand the connection between spirituality and mental health, but difficulties arise in determining which variable influenced the other.[12] More recent, sophisticated studies have found that considering a person's faith in mental health treatment often helps them heal faster and with longer-lasting outcomes.[13]

Still, this raises an important question. Do the people receiving help actually want to talk about their faith? That might be a complex question to answer, but guess who many people visit when they first experience symptoms of mental distress? Nearly a quarter of those struggling with mental illness seek help from their faith leader upon noticing symptoms—a higher percentage than those who go to a psychiatrist or medical doctor.[14] Although this could be due to financial barriers or a lack of access to certain providers, many of us don't recognize our experiences as symptoms of mental illness but rather assume they're only spiritual struggles.

Returning to the question about whether those receiving mental health treatment want to talk about their faith, some studies have suggested people often do want to discuss their spirituality in mental health care.[15] With generous support from the John Templeton Foundation in 2018, I decided to study this further and surveyed current clients across the United States about the intersection of spirituality and mental health.[16] The research team and I found that two-thirds of current mental health clients view their religion and spirituality as being relevant to their mental health *and* they want to talk about their faith as it relates to treatment. At least three out of five agreed that their spiritual practices improve their mental health, and their beliefs motivate them to seek ways to become mentally healthy. Of the other two out of five, one was neutral and the other disagreed.[17]

In addition, our research showed that most clients think it's important for their therapist to be competent in addressing religion and spirituality in their treatment.[18] These clients also report positive attitudes toward including their faith in mental health treatment. Roughly 70 percent were open to discussing their religious or spiritual beliefs in therapy and to working with a therapist who has a different belief system than they do. About as many clients also said a good therapist is sensitive to a client's religious or spiritual beliefs. Plus, these clients said their own beliefs are important to them during difficult times. (Further, about 20 percent had neutral responses to these statements and 10 percent disagreed with them.)

A growing body of research suggests that not only is there a relationship between spirituality and mental health, but when the client's or patient's spirituality is considered, it often leads to better outcomes than if it's disregarded.

So, How Does This Apply to Everyday Helpers?

Even though we're not all licensed therapists, understanding the connection between mental health and spirituality, and creating space for both journeys to coexist, allows us to better care for ourselves and for those around us. How do these journeys connect more practically with one another in our everyday lives? Let's consider the effects of spirituality on our everyday mental health.

Studies suggest collaborating with our higher power in healthy ways through life's difficulties leads to more positive mental health outcomes.[19] But research shows that not all of our views of God are the same or even positive. In fact, some researchers propose our views of God are mostly based on two continuums—engagement and judgment—resulting in us having generally four views of God: Authoritative (highly engaged with and highly judgmental of the world), Benevolent (high engagement, low judgment), Critical (low engagement, high judgment), and Distant (low engagement, low judgment).[20]

Do you know someone whose descriptions of God seem *completely* different from yours? Maybe one friend (who views God as Authoritative) regularly questions why God caused a painful circumstance to happen, while another (who views God as Benevolent) is more focused on how God cares for her by offering her support in times of need. It serves everyday helpers to understand how those they help might view God so they can hold space for the various views, both in themselves and for those they're trying to help.

As spiritual beings, we also experience spiritual struggles—including divine, demonic, interpersonal, moral, ultimate meaning, and doubt.[21] Researchers like Dr. Julie Exline and her team acknowledge that these struggles are often woven into our mental health journeys. And we know that spiritual trauma, which can sometimes be caused by a faith leader or faith community, may prompt those spiritual struggles. Although religion and spirituality include these areas of struggle, most of us view faith as a source of support and resilience. In fact, 93 percent of adults in the United States say that practicing their religion *helps* them gain comfort in times of trouble or sorrow.[22] So, it's important for everyday helpers to make room for the complexity of the spiritual journey of those they're helping, including the role of their higher power or God, their religious and spiritual beliefs, struggles, and practices.

But how do everyday helpers hold space for another's complex spiritual journey? First, we practice seeking the Sacred within ourselves. A diversity of spiritual practices exists across cultures and religious traditions that can help us connect with the Sacred while offering a sense of peace and hope. These may include prayer, meditation, yoga, centering prayer, singing, qigong, dancing, and Lectio Divina. Everyday practices also exist like gratitude, surrender, forgiveness, rest, mindfulness, deep breathing, creativity, patience, humility, and perhaps the most important for helpers: seeing our inherent belovedness and loving others as ourselves. By engaging in these practices, we become better acquainted with the Sacred in ourselves and humbly recognize these and other practices may be helpful for others. As helpers, we may even be able to support those we care for in discovering the unique spiritual practices that work for them.

Finally, and perhaps most importantly, we may have to unlearn the less healthy inner narratives. In the last few years it has become increasingly clear to me that many helpers operate from the core narrative that they aren't enough. This narrative undercuts our inherent worth and the belief that we are dearly beloved by God, just as we are. In other words, it's a narrative that shapes our belief in who we are in relation to God and can deeply impact our spiritual well-being and overall mental health.

We cannot love others well if we don't learn to love ourselves well, but this, too, is a journey. This isn't about pridefully viewing ourselves as *better* than others. Instead, it involves humbly recognizing that we cannot give to others what we haven't offered ourselves. I recognize how difficult this can be to read, having struggled most of my own life to truly love myself while still attempting to serve others. It wasn't until I realized how many subconscious strings were attached to my efforts to love others that I faced the soul-crushing truth that what I was offering others wasn't unconditional love. In the same way that we cannot pour from an empty cup, we cannot love others well if we are not practicing loving ourselves. And this takes intentional practice, just like a musical instrument or sport. We will feel discomfort and struggle through the awkward, fumbling, and wobbly efforts of practicing loving ourselves, but we will improve and grow through those efforts.

When we create space for our spiritual journey and mental health journey to coexist, we're better positioned to help those around us. When we allow ourselves the time to discern our views about our own deep spiritual beliefs, we can pay attention to and reduce imposing our assumptions, biases, and views of God onto those around us, including those we're helping. Without this kind of deep self-reflection, we may unintentionally hurt those around us.

So, how do we navigate all of this? We first turn to what's within so we can help those in the world around us. And for that, we turn to the Namaste Theory for helpers.

Reflection Exercises

Take a moment to reflect upon your own mental health journey. Are there times in your life when you needed extra support to cope with what you were experiencing? Are there others in your life whom you have walked alongside as they faced mental health struggles?

Take a moment to reflect upon your religious or spiritual beliefs and practices. How have your spiritual beliefs and practices impacted your mental health? (Also consider Drs. Froese & Bader's Four Gods as described in this chapter, and take their test at www.thearda.com/whoisyourgod.)

Do you see your mental health journey and spiritual journey as being connected positively, negatively, or a mixture of both? How have your experiences, surrounding environments, and social supports impacted either journey (or both)?

CHAPTER 3

Namaste Theory for Helpers

*Namaste helps us to break all the barriers in us
and to become humble. This in turn makes us
work as an instrument of God in the spiritual
or social fields of our activities.*[1]

—A. K. Krishna Nambiar

In 1967, Drs. Gordon Allport and Michael Ross postulated there were two poles of religiosity, one being intrinsic religiosity and the other being extrinsic religiosity. "The extrinsically motivated person," they wrote, "*uses* [their] religion, whereas the intrinsically motivated *lives* [their] religion."[2] In layman's terms, for the extrinsically religious, religion becomes a means to support their individual needs, such as security, comfort, social support, self-justification, or status. On the other hand, the intrinsically religious embrace, internalize, and fully live out their beliefs.

Describing intrinsic religiosity, Drs. Allport and Ross explain,

Persons with this orientation find their master motive in religion. Other needs, strong as they may be, are regarded as of less ultimate significance, and they are, so far as possible, brought into harmony with the religious beliefs and prescriptions. Having embraced a creed the individual endeavors to internalize it and follow it fully. It is in this sense that [they] *live* [their] religion.[3]

In other words, the intrinsically religious do not only believe what they say. They live it, embody it, and are motivated by it.

Over the course of my research, I've found that mental health care providers with higher degrees of intrinsic religiosity (regardless of their religious affiliation) are more inclined to consider the faith of the person they are trying to help. Their experiences of the Divine, the ways their beliefs motivate their whole approach to life, and how they carry their faith into everyday life impacts their attention and service to others, particularly when it comes to attending to clients' religion or spirituality.[4] This held true no matter the helper's age, race, gender, or the number of years the mental health care provider has been practicing. (Interestingly and importantly, receiving training in this topic was the second and only other predictor.)[5]

But not all mental health care providers consistently consider their clients' spiritual life. Simply put, while most have positive views about integrating clients' spirituality in therapy and don't see many barriers to it, far fewer are doing it.[6] Plus, we're learning there's little training happening in this area across disciplines.[7] And as I mentioned in the last chapter, considering clients' spirituality within their mental health treatment often improves outcomes. So these helpers' aversion to or avoidance of including clients' spirituality may be negatively impacting those they're seeking to serve.

From what I've read, learned, experienced, and gathered from conversations with others over time, this pattern seems to extend well beyond mental health care providers. Helpers with higher levels of intrinsic religiosity seem more comfortable and willing to consider the unique spiritual lives of those around them. If we want to holistically help those in the world around us, we must create space to nonjudgmentally explore our own unique spiritual landscape so we can hold the space for others to explore theirs as it relates to the ways we care for them.

For those of us who identify as more intrinsically religious (and if you're reading this book, you likely do), it is important to become more aware of and humbly grounded in what we believe. We also must become aware of how those beliefs intersect with our mental health and, truthfully, how this intersection trickles into what we do. If we aren't paying attention to this, we may find it difficult to hold the space needed for the spiritual and mental health journeys of those we serve.

This brings me to my operating thesis: *As helpers, we need to be curiously attentive and open to our dynamic inner landscape—including our spiritual and mental health journeys—as we engage in serving others, so that we can care for others from a place of sacred groundedness.* Put another way, we must recognize and heal what's within ourselves in order to truly recognize and heal what's within this world. To better understand why, let's turn to Namaste Theory.[8]

Namaste Theory

In 2017, while reviewing my own data and others' research findings, I noticed an emerging pattern. The mental health care provider's spirituality was a key factor when it came to considering the spirituality of those they served. It wasn't just that intrinsic religiosity was the top predictor of considering clients' faith. In response to an open-ended question, about half of the mental health care providers who participated in our study freely noted that elements of their own religion and spirituality supported them in considering their clients' faith.[9] And this wasn't just social workers. Psychologists, counselors, marriage and family therapists, and nurses responded the same way.[10] In other words, those whose spirituality is intimately tied to every aspect of their life were more inclined to see the Divine working in the lives of those they were helping.

One morning, while getting ready for work and considering the data, I had an "aha!" moment. A single word came to mind—*Namaste*—the Divine in me sees the Divine in you; the light in me sees the light in you; the Sacred in me sees the Sacred in you.[11] It was an epiphany, one that reshaped the way I viewed my research (and truthfully, everything) from that point forward.

Having practiced yoga before graduate school, I was loosely familiar with the term. I loved the moment in class when we folded our hands, bowed, and repeated "Namaste" to the instructor at the end. And though I knew *approximately* what it meant, I wanted to do a little more research after this epiphany to better understand, respect, and honor the origins of this word. So I turned to A. K. Krishna Nambiar's book, *Namaste: Its Philosophy and Significance in Indian Culture.*[12]

Nambiar explains Namaste's origins in the two Sanskrit words mentioned in the introduction, and writes the following about this Hindi term:

> *Namaste* recognises two forces that have ever existed in this world and suggests an effort on our part to bring these forces together in human relations. What are these two forces behind *Namaste*? They are Matter and Spirit.[13]
>
> . . . This gesture is an expression of humility: "I recognise God in you". If a human relationship begins with this feeling, can there be any room for crookedness and cunning in our dealings with each other? [HKO note: "Our dealings" include our desire and efforts to help.] . . .
>
> *Namaste* springs from great wisdom and its unfailing practice inculcates the feeling of "I recognise God in you" in one's relations with fellow beings—a feeling that almost becomes an instinct . . . [14]

... When it is extended to human beings it recognises the divinity in [humans] and thus [their] form is also recognised as the moving temple of God. . . . [15]

... *Namaste* in its true spirit helps our ego to surrender to the goal of our faith. . . . *Namaste* helps us to break all the barriers in us and to become humble. This in turn makes us work as an instrument of God in the spiritual or social fields of our activities. . . .

Though *Namaste* can be nourished and grown in any religious atmosphere, it ultimately helps us to transcend all limitations including the religious denomination under which we developed it. This is because *Namaste* aims at an integrated personality where heart and head are united in oneness. Therefore, *Namaste* removes all barriers that divide [human] and [human] and unites [humankind] in faith and wisdom. Ultimately, it is the faith and wisdom that will triumph over any sectarian practices in religions and finally religions themselves. And what we are in its evolutionary process actually experiencing in our development and progress through *Namaste* is knowledge. When this knowledge grows in faith, it becomes wisdom and this is the goal of the simple *Namaste* greeting and therefore it is equally applicable to everybody alike, irrespective of caste, creed, colour or nationality.

Once matter and spirit are integrated in a personality, *Namaste* helps to reveal love.[16]

This acknowledgement of the Divine or Sacred within both ourselves and others brought order and understanding to what I saw emerging in my data across helping professions. So I reoriented my research around this term, and in 2017, I developed and published this quantitative grounded theory, Namaste Theory, explaining,

As practitioners experience, are engaged in, become aware of, and infuse their own religious/spiritual beliefs and practices into their daily lives—deepening their intrinsic religiosity and becoming more attuned to the sacred within—they tend to hold more positive views and engage in clients' religious/spiritual beliefs and practices as well. In other words, as helping professionals recognize the sacred within themselves, they appear to be more open to recognizing the sacred within their client.[17]

Before we move on, let's explore the term *Sacred*. What is it? As I use the term, I mean "a person, an object, a principle, or a concept that transcends the self. Though the Sacred may be found within the self, it has perceived value independent of the self. Perceptions of the Sacred invoke feelings of respect, reverence, devotion and may, ideally, serve an integrative function in human personality."[18] Understanding the term *Sacred* in this way allows the element of "sacred" within Namaste to be more inclusive, especially for those who identify as atheist or agnostic. What I may call God or the Divine, others may call Mystery, Love, Light, Universe, or Higher Power. The more we become deeply aware of and grounded within these areas of our lives, the more comfortable we are in holding space for others to explore this area within their own lives.

Namaste Theory for Everyday Helpers

As I've further studied this topic, I've realized that Namaste Theory is applicable to helpers in general. In speaking with a diverse array of fellow helpers, I've found that something immediately resonates or "clicks" when I bring up the theory in conversation. Inevitably, their faces soften, they say something along the lines of "ohhh, that makes sense," and they share how another's grounded view of the Divine has impacted their own spiritual and mental health journey. Likewise, they'll share a time when their grounded faith allowed them to be fully present to someone who needed their help, even if that person didn't share the helper's belief system.

Practicing Namaste Theory allows us to transcend the typical walls of division, as Nambiar noted above, moving us toward the process of seeking the Sacred. It allows us to lovingly address and integrate the taboo topics of spirituality and mental health, which we know through research are connected.

As we will discuss in the following chapters, Namaste Theory has practical implications for our own lives. It offers us the framework we need to fill up our well by recognizing the Sacred within ourselves so that we can serve from a place of wholeness and abundance. In this way, it allows us to avoid imposing our beliefs on others, hurting others in our efforts to help, or serving with strings attached. It helps us understand just how *enough* we are, how *loved* we are, so that we can share that love with our neighbors. As theologian and professor Fr. Henri Nouwen writes, with a nod to this idea of loving our neighbor *as* ourselves:

> The more you learn to love God, the more you learn to know and to cherish yourself. Self-knowledge and self-love are the fruit of knowing and loving God. You can see better now what is intended by the great commandment to "love the Lord your God with all your heart, with all your soul, and with all your mind, and to love your neighbor as yourself." Laying our hearts totally open to God leads to a love of ourselves that enables us to give wholehearted love to our fellow human beings. In the seclusion of our hearts we learn to know the hidden presence of God; and with that spiritual knowledge we can lead a loving life.[19]

Looking Ahead: The Seven-Stage Journey of Seeking the Sacred

In light of Namaste Theory, my research findings suggest helpers who are more grounded in their spirituality and motivated to live out their faith are more likely to consider the spiritual journey of those they're trying to help. These helpers are less threatened by and less reactive to others' beliefs. Helpers who align with Namaste Theory (even if they're unaware of it) aren't unconsciously longing to work out their religious and spiritual beliefs with those they are caring for or trying to help. Instead, they actively honor the Sacred that is present in the other.

Namaste Theory begins with seeking the Sacred in ourselves so that we can see it in others. It's a process that emerged as I began to understand and integrate the research into my own life. In Part II, we'll build upon the initial grounded theory and explore it in more detail, moving through this journey of seeking the Sacred in ourselves and others as a seven-stage process or model to embody Namaste Theory.

Speed: In this first stage, we awaken to our speed, to the fact that the default pace of our lives is *go, go, go*. We continually help, serve, and care for others, even to the exclusion of our own health. Left unchecked, our seemingly noble efforts and fast pace can distract us from seeing the Sacred in ourselves and others.

Slow: After recognizing the speed at which we've been operating, our next step is to take the foot off the accelerator. It's as simple and as excruciatingly hard as that. Learning to slow our pace allows us the margin to see the Sacred within ourselves.

Steady: When we slow down, discomfort emerges. We come face to face with some of our deepest fears. Do we worry that we're unworthy, unloved, or unimportant? Are these the fears that motivated us to hustle and strive in the first place? In this stage, we adopt practices that hold us steady in the tension and help us begin to heal.

Still: Having resisted the urge to accelerate, we become still within ourselves. When we are still, we fully see. We understand how the pace of our lives blurred our vision. Once still, we can know the presence of God within us (Psalm 46:10).

See: Stilled to the world around us (and our own efforts), we begin to see the Divine in us. We comprehend it. We're open to fully receiving our inherent birthright as beloved children of God and beloved siblings of one another. And once we see, we can't unsee.

Shift: As deeply motivated and changed as we may feel upon waking up to the Sacred within, change takes time. Without intention and attention, it can be easy to put our foot back on the accelerator. Two shifts toward compassion occur in this phase. The first is within our entire being toward ourselves when we see the Sacred within. The second is toward others, recognizing each of us bears the image of God within too.

Serve: As we see the divine spark within ourselves and others, we move toward serving from a place of abundance, awareness, and attention. We're better able to discern our work, our capacity, our boundaries, and our motivations. Knowing we're fully loved just as we are, we're better positioned to serve unconditionally without seeking affirmation, accolades, or affection.

We cannot force or hurry or checklist our way through this journey. Instead, we must position ourselves to navigate these seven stages to the best of our ability with curiosity, humility, and a budding trust that the Divine will lead us.

Are you ready to take this first step along this seven-stage journey? Come along. Namaste.

Reflection Exercises

As you read about intrinsic and extrinsic religiosity, did you find yourself identifying with either (or neither) term in this season of life? If one resonated more for you, are there previous seasons when the other term was more descriptive of your experiences?

Prior to this chapter, had you heard of the term Namaste? What was the context in which you heard about it, and what did you understand about that term? Has anything changed in your understanding of it after reading this chapter?

Reflect on the above seven-stage journey of seeking the Sacred. What resonates? Is there any emotion, thought, or sensation that has surfaced for you to name and hold space for before moving into Part II?

PART II

The Journey of Seeking the Sacred

Finding the Sacred Within Ourselves to See It in Others

CHAPTER 4

Speed

No matter how fast you run,
your shadow more than keeps up.[1]

—Rumi

"So, what you're saying is I can either forgo maternity leave, continue my research assistant position, and keep my insurance, *or* I can take six weeks of unpaid leave? And if I take the leave, I wouldn't have an income and would need to pay *more* for insurance?"

"Yes, ma'am," the HR representative replied.

I was in the last semester of my PhD coursework and six months pregnant with our daughter, Callie. We couldn't afford to lose my $1,100 monthly stipend nor was there any money to pay higher insurance rates. The alternative—returning to work within days of giving birth—was also unthinkable. Cory and I were only a year into marriage, both enrolled in school, barely making enough money to pay our bills (and sometimes not enough), transitioning into parenthood, and now we were facing what felt like an impossible decision.

"Fine," I said to the HR representative, recognizing this wasn't her fault but a broader, systemic issue. Still, I was fuming inside. "I'll talk with my supervisor and figure something out," I said before hanging up. I'm sure she heard my voice trembling.

Thankfully, my supervisor understood the situation and worked with me to create a plan that would at least allow a two- to three-week break. But the plan was ambitious. I would need to log some extra hours for my research assistant position before Callie was born to allow the time. Then I'd set out to finish my PhD coursework in May, complete my comprehensive exam in June, and propose my dissertation in July. I'd give birth in August, take a few weeks off, then go back to the grind. To sum it up, I'd do what I'd always done to bring a sense of safety and security. I'd point my nose in the direction of work and I'd put the pedal to the metal. It seemed to be the only choice I had.

I worked the plan, logged my advanced hours, finished my coursework, passed my comprehensive exam, and successfully defended my dissertation proposal. Come August, I went into labor, had Callie, and within a few weeks was back to work. Thankfully, my supervisor continued to be as flexible and supportive as possible. But I wasn't sleeping or adjusting well in those early months, and I struggled with postpartum depression and anxiety. And through it all, I kept pushing, partially afraid of what others would think if I slowed down, partially mindful of a system that didn't support me slowing down, and partially afraid of the anxiety that might surface if I wasn't remaining busy. But ignoring my insecurity and anxiety didn't make it go away. Instead, it only worsened.

Was I doing enough to make my boss happy, to keep the job I needed to provide for my family?

Was my dissertation work good enough and was I on track with the timeline?

Was I laying the groundwork for a career that would finally pay the bills and be helpful to others?

Meanwhile, insecurities about whether I was a good mom began surfacing.

Was I cultivating a secure attachment with Callie?

Could I keep her safe and healthy?

Was I reading to her enough or bringing her to enough playdates?

A sort of dizzying confusion set in over those first months. The whiplash of feeling deep gratitude for the opportunities and roles I juggled alongside mounting pressure and shame over feeling like I wasn't doing enough in each area was simply too much. The competing and increasing demands that others expected from me (and that I expected from myself) left me feeling helpless and stuck. And no matter how hard I pressed, I couldn't seem to make everything balance.

Ten months after Callie's birth, I was lying facedown on the living room floor, sobbing in defeat. I was at the end of my rope, tired of all the planning, working, people-pleasing, and performing. Something had to give, but I had no idea what. In fact, I was left with more questions than answers.

Why is my plate always so full?

Why do I always take on more than I can manage?

What am I trying to hide or cover up or avoid facing by keeping myself so busy?

Unable to answer those questions, I pushed them aside and kept going. Maybe if I just hustled a little more, achieved a little more, or better organized my planner, things would fall into place. Maybe I'd finally get everything done on my plate, be able to rest, and be seen as enough.

Looking back, I can see how I was attempting to earn a sense of security, worth, and belonging through all that work. Fr. Henri Nouwen explains this insatiable need to earn belonging through productivity well (italics added for emphasis):

I do not want to suggest that productivity is wrong or needs to be despised. On the contrary, productivity and success can greatly enhance our lives. But when our value as human beings depends on what we make with our hands and minds, we become victims of the fear tactics of our world. *When productivity is our main way of overcoming self-doubt, we are extremely vulnerable to rejection and criticism and prone to inner anxiety and depression. Productivity can never give the deep sense of belonging we crave. The more we produce, the more we realize that successes and results cannot give us the experience of "at homeness." In fact, our productivity often reveals to us that we are driven by fear.*[2]

The Fast and the Furious

Our world moves at such a breakneck speed. We caffeinate, go, hurry, schedule, hustle, charge, push, and rush at an inhuman pace. We've enshrined this notion of speed into our language: instant coffee, overnight delivery, speed dating, fast charging stations, express lanes, high-speed Internet. We are always on, constantly hustling, relentlessly busy, and perpetually plugged in. Oriented toward speed while valuing efficiency, we stay stuck in go mode. It's often our way of *being* in the world.

As you might have noted in the opening story of this chapter, I've struggled with an addiction to speed and productivity, often believing that doing more (especially when it's tied to helping others) will lead to more efficiency, achievements, admiration, and ultimately, acceptance. I've believed that if I hustled twice as hard as I'm expected to, I might prove my enoughness and avoid rejection. Some of this is based on both systemic and individual narratives I've picked up and internalized along the way, while some is based on my own personality's tendencies and present circumstances. Truthfully, when my plate begins to fill fast, I can easily still fall into that thought process. (Does any of this sound familiar?)

But do we have to prove our enoughness? No. We are enough by virtue of our creation. Enoughness came prepackaged deep within us, even before we took our first breath. How do I know? Because, as I'll share later in this chapter, I came to experience this truth firsthand in my teens. I came to understand that we've been created with the divine spark within us. This divine spark exists regardless of what we've done in our lives, the choices we've made, the people we've known, or the ways we've flat-out failed or soaringly succeeded. And it's that piece of Sacredness within us that connects us with the Divine. It's that piece that constantly whispers, "You are beloved, just as you are."

It is a simple truth, but this experience of being human is terribly difficult. After all, we're born into a system that teaches us we are what we do and ties our worth to our accomplishments and productivity. But what if we believed we were inherently enough? Would that give us the freedom to slow down and contemplate a different way of living?

Stuck in Precontemplation—Why We Can't See Our Speed

In the early 1980s, Drs. James Prochaska and Carlo DiClemente published one of today's most widely recognized models when it comes to addiction and behavioral science: the Stages of Change Model, also known as the Transtheoretical Model.[3] These psychologists suggested there are six stages to achieving lasting change: precontemplation, contemplation, preparation, action, maintenance, and termination. If you run in recovery circles, there's a good chance you've come across these stages before. They're often used to help those with addictions change undesirable behaviors.

Though each stage is necessary for behavioral change, let's focus on precontemplation. In this stage, we're often unaware our behavior is problematic. We lack the motivation to change and see no real reason for it. And when it comes to addictive tendencies—especially the addiction to the high-speed pace of our lives—most of us hang out in the precontemplation stage for a very long time.

Why?

Hustling and hurrying, especially when linked to helping others, are often rewarded. And it's that reward that allows us to justify our pace. Like any other addictive behavior—drinking, gambling, shopping, even checking social media—we might promise we'll slow down, but when we receive the reward (whether financial, physiological, or emotional), we rationalize our behavior. We believe our work and efforts to help ultimately make us worthy, bring security, or offer a sense of acceptance or appreciation. And so we stay in the precontemplation stage, and we keep chasing.

It's easy to hang out in the precontemplation stage, refusing to face the problems caused by our behaviors. I still catch myself taking on too much without thinking about it. The result? After an overly busy day, I'll crash on the couch, worn out and depleted. There, without much mental margin to discern what I really need to recover from the busy day, I'll turn to more negative coping mechanisms. I might mindlessly scroll through social media. I might respond to emails late into the evening. I might binge-watch a few episodes of *This Is Us*. Prior to December 2019, it wasn't uncommon to end such a day with a glass of wine . . . or three. And though these behaviors in moderation might be fine, when I engage them excessively and without thought—that is, in the precontemplation stage—as a way to numb the stress or pain, they are problematic.

Although I believe we are all doing the best we can with what we have, can you see how one unhealthy behavior leads to others? Considering these tendencies to mindlessly cope with the speed of our lives, what might be a healthier way to deal with the effects of and recover from our fast pace? Perhaps rather than binge-watching, drinking, emailing, or scrolling at the end of a hard day, it may be more healing to get curious about why we're so tired. Perhaps we should ask ourselves why our pace is so fast or why we're pressing so hard.

We cannot move from precontemplation to contemplation (that is, taking a hard look at our unhealthy behaviors and beginning to consider the need to change them) if we don't slow down long enough to evaluate our behaviors. So why don't we? Maybe we think slowing down isn't safe, that the speed of our life gives us the financial, social, professional, or even spiritual security we're seeking. Maybe we're afraid we'll lose an opportunity, be forgotten, or rejected. Put another way, we are afraid we'll discover we are not enough. (That said, I recognize there are seasons in which many of us must hustle to survive, often while navigating systemic issues, nodding to my experience in the opening story. Slowing down might not be an option, but my hope is there's a clear difference between a temporary high-speed pace to survive versus a constant, long-term hustling for our worth.)

Whatever the reason, many of us are moving through life as if a fire is two inches from our tail, not even considering that slowing down is an option. We are running ragged, exhausted from pushing so hard and so fast for so long, doing as much as we can for as many people as we can, hooked onto everyone else's expectations of us to obtain their approval.

This is no way to live. Period.

When we don't slow down to assess our pace and the reasons for it, we risk so much. We risk falling into other addictions, as I indicated above. We risk falling into devastating burnout. Ultimately, we risk hurting those we love and serve.

Moving at the Speed of Burnout

Throughout the COVID-19 pandemic, the word *burnout* became increasingly common in our vocabulary. But even before 2020, so many of us felt the onset of burnout. And though some flippantly use this term to describe fatigue or the feeling following a rough day, the reality is that we really are burning out faster than we once were, particularly among helpers.

In 2019, the World Health Organization (WHO) updated its definition of burnout, calling it a "syndrome conceptualized as resulting from chronic workplace stress that has not been successfully managed."[4] The WHO further notes that burnout includes three dimensions:

- Feelings of energy depletion or exhaustion
- Increased mental distance from one's job, or feelings of negativism or cynicism related to one's job
- Reduced professional efficacy

In 2018, Gallup completed a study of 7,500 full-time employees. The findings were astounding: 44 percent "sometimes" felt burned out, and another 23 percent "often" or "always" felt burned out.[5] And when it comes to those in helping professions, the numbers are even higher. In 2018, 78 percent of physicians experienced feelings of burnout, which has only risen in recent years due to growing administrative responsibilities, decreased time with patients, and the growing stress from the COVID-19 pandemic.[6] In my own 2013 study of social workers across the United States, most of whom were in private practice, 60 percent reported mild to severe symptoms of burnout.[7] Even within my diverse 2015 sample of helping professionals in Texas (including nurses, counselors, psychologists, marriage and family therapists, and social workers), 69 percent reported mild to severe symptoms of burnout.[8]

This rising issue of burnout extends to nonprofessional helpers too. In 2019, an article in *Clinical Psychological Science* reported that parental burnout can result in neglect, escape ideation, and violence toward children.[9] The authors of the article noted that about 3.5 million parents struggled with parental burnout.[10] Again, these numbers were before parents were asked to juggle the impossible load of working full-time jobs at home (or facing unemployment) while caregiving, teaching their children, learning virtual platforms, navigating complex emotions and trauma, and tending to the mounting personal responsibilities that came with the COVID-19 pandemic.[11] I'm convinced that if the study were repeated today, the numbers would be far higher.

Many of us are facing ever-increasing pressures and responsibilities, competing demands from others, and very real reasons to neglect our boundaries in our efforts to provide the critical care others need. Though helping others is truly noble, good, and desperately needed in today's world, burnout disrupts this work. It leaves us without energy to tend to our own spiritual and mental health journeys. It leaves us unable to tend to the Sacred within us. Ultimately, it leaves us unable to serve the Sacred in others. But why are helpers so prone to burnout?

Primary and Secondary Stress—Contributors to Burnout

The iconic Fred Rogers recounted a story about seeing scary news events during his childhood:

> My mother would say to me, "Look for the helpers. You will always find people who are helping." To this day, especially in

times of "disaster," I remember my mother's words, and I am always comforted by realizing that there are still so many helpers—so many caring people in this world.[12]

Helpers are so important within the fabric of our shared humanity. They bring healing to the pain and brokenness of the world by their acts of service. It's nothing short of a divine calling to commit one's life to being a helper, regardless of our job title or task. But that divine calling comes with its own pressures and occupational hazards, especially when we're working within organizations and systems that don't recognize or support healing from those occupational hazards.

As we help others, we will hear excruciatingly painful stories or bear witness to traumatic experiences. And because of the messiness of life, many helpers hear these stories over and over and over again. It's these stories that bring on different kinds of stress—primary stress and secondary stress.

Primary stress injuries are directly experienced by the helper and include acute stress or post-traumatic stress. Secondary stress injuries—those experienced by helpers who empathize with others who have experienced the primary stress injuries—include compassion fatigue, secondary traumatic stress, and vicarious trauma.

Compassion fatigue, which many helpers are at risk of experiencing, is the "cost of caring."[13] It could aptly be described as empathetic exhaustion and is "bearing the suffering of [others] and the natural consequent behaviors and emotions resulting from knowing about a traumatizing event experienced or suffered by a person."[14] Further, some have described compassion fatigue as multi-dimensional, involving both acute secondary traumatic stress and a gradual emotional exhaustion through burnout.[15]

Secondary traumatic stress and vicarious trauma are similar but distinct. Secondary trauma is a result of hearing the details of a traumatic event from someone who experienced it. Vicarious trauma is experienced by helpers whose sense of self and worldview are negatively transformed from the *continual* exposure to victims of violence and trauma.[16] Both are the indirect effects of another's trauma, including those we serve, and these hazards can extensively impact our mental, emotional, physical, and spiritual health. When not tended to, these forms of secondary (and sometimes primary) stress contribute to burnout, particularly when we don't slow down long enough to notice and name the mounting stress and trauma, let alone heal from it.

Why We Overheat

Just as an engine can overheat from working too hard for too long, so do we, and we are both much more fragile and more resilient than an engine. That's why paying attention to the occupational hazards of being a helper—especially related to mental health and trauma—is critical. It's why it's important to mind our tendencies toward speed, hustle, and hurry. Because if we operate at an unsustainable speed, trying too hard to prove our worth while taking on too much trauma, we'll eventually burn out.

So, ask yourself: Why do we tend to ignore our burnout and keep pushing?

In his book *Falling Upward*, Fr. Richard Rohr writes that at some point in our lives, what once worked for us no longer does.[17] We begin to see that the compulsive behaviors we once used to avoid the pain of not being enough and to "gain" a sense of belonging no longer serve us. When these tactics fall short, we tend to hustle more, press more, perform more, people-please more, and try to achieve more. But if we take the time to slow down and be honest with ourselves, we'll awaken to the truth that none of these things are leading us to health and wholeness. Things *must* change if we're to be healthy and whole. These kinds of moments bring opportunities for transition, and it's up to us to accept the opportunity to the best of our ability and discern what our next step might be.

It's up to us to be reflective through the process and extend grace toward ourselves through these moments of transition, remembering we genuinely believed (consciously or not) that our breakneck pace was necessary in order to survive, obtain security, or be safe. We did the best we could, engaging each day with the information, experiences, coping skills, and discernment we had, but that old speed will no longer do. So we need to take the time to ask what's behind the pace, including what our motivations were behind it. Consider my own reflection, for instance.

Longing for Enoughness

Although I do have lots of positive memories woven into my childhood, I also was exposed to and survived an unbelievable amount of trauma. My biological father was emotionally, verbally, and physically abusive. My mother was understandably preoccupied with our family's safety, and though she was incredibly supportive, protective, and loving toward me and my sister (and created a safe and stable home for healing in my teens), she was not always mentally or emotionally available. The result of such inconsistent support and pain alongside the complexity of so many good, heartbreaking, joyful, and traumatic memories? I absolutely lacked a secure attachment with my biological father, and at times I struggled in my attachment with my mother too.

My own lack of safe and consistent attachment, the painful experiences, and the reoccurring rejection from my biological father threaded throughout my childhood led me to wonder whether I was enough, whether I was loved. This wondering led me to believe that if I could do more, especially for others, I could prove my self-worth. And doing more meant adopting an unsustainable pace. Thankfully, God would meet me in a middle school Passion performance and offer a reminder I'd need to recall later in life.

At the Catholic middle school I attended, the eighth graders had an annual performance called the *Passion Mime* held during Holy Week. Each student dressed as a silent mime—we wore black and painted our faces white with some small symbols—and silently acted out the Stations of the Cross. Students were selected to represent Jesus, Mother Mary, Mary Magdalene, Barabbas, Pontius Pilate, and to read the sacred text through the service.

The director who led us through practice each week created space for us to marinate in the sacred texts of this historical event. We read scripture about the last week of Jesus's life, felt the emotions of that week, and then embodied the Passion by acting it out. It was a full body-mind-heart-soul meditation that this group of about fifty eighth graders could experience while seeing our friends in these roles.

The truth is, I didn't care much about the spiritual formation aspects of the production. Like any other fourteen-year-old girl, I was more motivated by the social aspect and the fact that my most recent crush would be at each gathering. But the week before the actual performance, something shifted and clicked as we practiced. *I understood.*

As one of my closest friends, Emily, read the sacred text during our final practice, I watched another friend, Jon, straight-faced and somber, contemplatively act out Jesus's final days as we followed the movements of the crowd that week. He entered Jerusalem on Palm Sunday, was arrested, judged, nailed to the cross, and hung. After he breathed his last breath, he was laid on a door and carried around the sanctuary as we all grieved. Although this was a performance, in that moment I noticed a deep, heavy, piercing stirring within the center of my chest. It felt foreign. And as the practice concluded, as we made our way to the back of the sanctuary in single file, I did the only thing I could in that moment: I wept.

Looking straight ahead in a transcendent daze, the stirring became clear, and I thought: *Someone I've never met was willing to sacrifice his life so that I could wake up and know who God is. He fully surrendered his life for others and knowingly took on more pain than I will ever know or experience because he loves me.* And it wasn't just me he loved. It was all of us, all of humanity.

Thank God for this awkward, fully organic and embodied middle school prayer service, which resurrected a new hope of faith from the broken religious messages I received as a child. The trauma continued at home, but I began to shake off the pieces of religion that no longer fit with what my soul had experienced. Slowly, I began to believe that I was enough, regardless of my home life, regardless of the rules, regardless of the ways I didn't measure up.

That day I came to understand that I didn't need to earn this love I had experienced. Instead, I was worthy of love just by the very nature of being God's child, and I didn't have to do a single thing to earn it or receive it. Still, as I grew and continued to cope with my family's situation and with the mounting pressures of life, I lost sight of this fact. I wouldn't experience this depth of love again until early adulthood, until I learned that I had to slow down to experience the fullness of this love.

Losing Sight of Love and Discovering the Accelerator

This vulnerable epiphany—knowing we are loved by God just as we are and that there's nothing we can do to be more loved—is what I think Jesus is referring to when he describes childlike faith. But I do not think this experience is limited to those who identify as

Christian. Other faith traditions and spiritual guides teach similar messages. The notion of this kind of Divine Love is present in a tapestry of diverse forms.

After my mom remarried, my dad (my stepfather who adopted me as an adult) and I would have conversations late into the evening about this beautiful thread of Divine Love that weaves through religious traditions. Although we were coming from different traditions—my dad identified as Buddhist—we always approached the conversation with deep respect of the other's belief system, a genuine love for one another, and a desire to learn with a curiosity and appreciation for the Divine Love within the other.

Unfortunately, as I aged, I armored up to protect my heart in the ways I had as a child, despite what I knew about the God who loved me regardless of my performance. I still longed to be seen as competent and accepted. I longed for safety and security too. I even longed for a sense of control over my time and tasks. So I did what so many of us do: I found my accelerator, pushed the gas pedal down, and hustled.

The truth is, I thought doing more would prove my worth and help me to feel a sense of love and belonging. And so I found myself moving at a breakneck speed, even in the name of helping and serving others, and stress set in. Pain set in. Burnout set in.

That's when I realized I had a choice to make. I could keep my foot on the accelerator, or I could take it off.

Reflection Exercises

Do you find yourself moving too fast at times? Do you try to pack too much into each hour of each day? Spend some time reflecting on why you move at the pace you do.

Have you experienced any of the occupational hazards of being a helper? In what ways, if any, are burnout, secondary trauma, vicarious trauma, or compassion fatigue a part of your journey as a helper?

Draw a picture of a foot pressing down on an accelerator. Scribble down some immediate words, phrases, or images of what is keeping your foot attached to the accelerator. For example, is it the approval and expectations of others, financial security, or the internal need to prove something? Thinking about the pressures you listed, name the fears that are keeping your foot attached to that accelerator and preventing you from taking it off.

CHAPTER 5

Slow

Can we handle the busy? Can we handle a quicker
pace, a heftier load? Perhaps we were never intended
to. God will not give us more than we can handle,
the saying goes. But what does it say about what
we give ourselves? What then?[1]

—Erin Loechner

As I began my second year at Baylor in the fall of 2015, my plate began to fill. Fast. I was teaching three classes—a PhD-level research methods class that met for three hours one night a week and two sections of an undergraduate statistics class that met three days a week. I was working on four separate research studies. One explored the views of spirituality among young adults with serious mental illness.[2] One examined how Christian social workers integrated their faith into their social work practice.[3] One surveyed U.S. adults' views of God, religious coping, and preferences for integrating their faith into mental health care.[4] And one assessed Texas helping professionals' views about integrating spirituality in mental health treatment.[5]

I was also grieving the death of our school's beloved dean, Dr. Diana Garland, while participating in meetings for our search for a new dean.[6] I traveled regularly to present at professional conferences, and I was always behind on my emails. I was serving on six committees within my school and a couple of others outside my school. I was writing book reviews, volunteering as a peer reviewer for research articles and conference proposals, consulting on others' research studies, mentoring students, and nominating colleagues for awards. And I was still learning the tenure-track process, trying my best to meet every explicit and implicit requirement.

Most importantly, I was also in my last trimester of carrying our son, Oliver. And because I was the first faculty member in our school to navigate the tenure-track process while pregnant (my second tenure review was that October), I couldn't shake the unwritten rule I'd heard over the years: women shouldn't have children during their tenure-track years because it was too much of a distraction from their work. Thankfully, the faculty at Baylor refused to give space to that unwritten rule. They allowed me twelve weeks of paid leave to bond with Oliver, heal from the delivery and lack of sleep, and adjust to new family realities.

Looking back, this paid leave gave me the most holy and sacred gift of space. As with the birth of our daughter, Callie, I endured another bout of postpartum depression and anxiety after Oliver was born. There were sleepless nights and sleep-deprived fights with Cory. There were unforeseen adjustments that came with our second child, especially without nearby family around to help. Still, in that break provided by my university, I had nothing to do but *be* in the moment.

At the same time, I felt a curious pressure to continue my research because I didn't want to disrupt the tenure clock, especially as the sole financial provider of our family. And more to the point, the idea of slowing anything down—my pace, my research, my career—was uncomfortable for more than financial reasons. I struggled with not being needed by colleagues or students. I was uneasy with not having an endless to-do list, a list of things to distract me from my feelings of inadequacy.

Regardless of whether I'd admit it, I was afraid of slowing down. And those fears were becoming more and more real as the weeks passed. Somewhere toward the end of the semester, I took those fears to Cory and some friends, who helped me understand the nature of my fear.

I was afraid of how others viewed me while on leave.

I was afraid of how to prove my worth without being productive.

I was afraid of being forgotten, unneeded, and irrelevant to my colleagues.

I was afraid of what was buried deep beneath the decades of hustling.

I was afraid of operating at any other speed besides GO.

I was afraid of what would happen if I slowed down.

And as I wrestled with those fears throughout Oliver's first year, three books crossed my path: Shauna Niequist's *Present Over Perfect*, Rachel Macy Stafford's *Hands Free Life*, and Erin Loechner's *Chasing Slow*.[7] These books woke me up to the ways I used work to prove my self-worth, the ways I used social media to supplement that self-worth, and the ways I used other coping mechanisms to numb myself from past pain that caused me to question my self-worth in the first place. They led me to step away from these coping mechanisms and be more fully present to the people I'd been entrusted to love, including myself. They helped me awaken to my one, precious, and sacred life and to what I was at risk of losing if I didn't disconnect from my numbing tactics, slow down, and stop trying to prove I was enough.

The margin Baylor gave me in the spring of 2016 and the following summer break allowed me the space I needed to notice and face my fears with a sense of safety and curiosity. It helped me move from precontemplation to contemplation as I read, reflected, and explored the benefits of a slower pace. In that time, I slowed down enough to begin hearing that still, small voice of God like I did in the eighth grade. Ultimately, it planted the seeds of courage I needed for what was ahead.

Begin with Awareness and Being Present

Have you ever wondered about the shift in our orientation to time as we age? As kids, we often play, create, imagine, daydream, and soak up all of the beauty and miracles this world offers us without worrying too much about *work* or what we need to *do*. We take the time to marvel at everything—dandelions, butterflies, a thick carpet of grass. We take the time to become friends with all sorts of people, too, regardless of any of their layers of intersectionality. As kids, we are really good at the "being" part of "human being."

Over time, this changes. So many of us take in the toxic message that our self-worth and security are measured by our productivity, service, and achievements. We stop "being" and shift into "doing" to support an unconscious illusion that we can avoid pain in this life.

As we engage in this world as "human doings," we lose sight of the present moment. Dandelions are just weeds to remove. Butterflies are just insects to ignore. Grass just keeps growing, adding yet another chore to tackle by mowing the lawn. There's no time to marvel when there are "more important" things to *do*. And that's to say nothing of tending to and paying attention to our own fears, anxieties, and pains.

Attach all that "doing" to a noble cause, one that's affirmed by others, and it becomes easily justified. And when we justify our speed, when we don't slow down, we will begin to miss the sacred threads within the unpromised moment. We'll miss opportunities to examine our own mental and emotional landscape. We'll miss the beauty, goodness, and truth around us. We'll miss God, God's love for us, and where God is showing up in both the pain and joy of life.

If there's one thing I learned in the season after giving birth to Oliver, it's that slowing down gave me the space I needed to radically reexamine my life. That's why I'm convinced now more than ever: we must slow down. To do that, we need to awaken to the truth that we are enough regardless of how much we do (or don't do). As helpers and healers, we must engage this world differently than the surrounding high-speed pace and impulsive tendencies to take on more than we realistically can. We must receive our belovedness as an invitation to a different sort of pace. We need to rest in deeply knowing our inherent worth and humbly trust that we, as human beings, have limits. Why? Because this slower speed helps us avoid burnout, maintain our health, and gives us time and energy to connect with the Divine within and around us.

Believe me, I know life is hard with its endless pressures and stressors, but during your brief life, while you are here with us, please *be present*. Be with God. Allow God to be with you. Be with us. Allow us to be with you. Be with yourself. Journal. Reflect. Slow down and pray. Sit with your children. Snuggle with your partner. Hold space for your friends and loved ones. Listen to your students and teachers. Receive the gift of rest and the gift of *your life*. After all, how can you help others be present to God, themselves, and those around them if you are not practicing these yourself?

Baby Steps to Slowing Down

Let's go back to the image of your foot being attached to the accelerator and begin to imagine what it might look like to slowly ease off the gas. Start by feeling your foot on the accelerator. What weight is keeping it there? Is there some occupational pressure, fear, need for power or control, or potential addiction? Name it.

If you're like me, the weight pressing on your foot might be hard to name. Some words might flicker into your mind and then quickly dance away because you don't want to face them or because it's too scary or because distractions surface. Still, to the best of your ability, try to stay with it. Be patient with yourself and gently hold the space you need to identify why you keep pressing down on the accelerator. Then ask yourself, what does this weight feel like? Is it causing you stress, anxiety, or worry to even consider it? How fast are you going *because* of it?

Now, recognize a simple truth: You will not be able to take your foot off the accelerator without releasing that weight holding your foot down. And you may not really want to. You may have gotten used to this weight, this speed, the shaking and shuddering as you reach a pace that feels almost out of control. You've become comfortable with this discomfort. But what happens when you can no longer control the speed? What happens if you lose control, or hurt someone, or run off the road? What happens if you run the gas tank dry?

At the same time, you might be more concerned about what you'll find when you slow down. You might come face to face with some deeper inner fear or pain, like your feelings of inadequacy or the sense that you're not enough. You might wonder whether you'll be able to provide financial security for your family or whether you're doing enough work to get ahead in or keep your job. You may be afraid others won't feel loved if you're not constantly giving them attention. Maybe you wonder whether you'll be remembered if you aren't hustling to be known.

These are just some of the questions that surface when we slow down, questions the world teaches us to ask about our self-worth and belonging. No wonder these existential questions motivate us to go faster and harder, not knowing the long-term consequences or how to be once we slow down.

A Word About the Ways We Use Shame

It can be scary to exist in the world at a countercultural pace. But there's an ancillary truth that's worth pointing out. If we don't slow down, we'll likely shame others into keeping our same breakneck pace.

As part of my master's in social work program, I took Dr. Brené Brown's "Shame, Empathy, and Resilience" class in 2010 at the University of Houston. About a week in, I realized an important truth that left me curled up on a couch, crushed, crying my eyes out. After I composed myself, I called Cory—then my fiancé—and apologized between heart-ripping sobs and brutal vulnerability. My own battle with shame was spilling over into my relationship with him.

To combat the messages of inadequacy and worthlessness I'd received throughout my life, I internalized surrounding unrealistic standards and imposed them upon myself. I shamed myself, thinking that by meeting certain benchmarks, I'd eventually rest in enoughness, and hustling was just part of the process. I subconsciously set the same standard for those around me, including Cory. In some ways, it came out as sincerely cheering on his efforts toward healthy striving. (For example, encouraging him to keep going with his college courses when he wanted to quit.) But in a lot of ways, I took the message of worth being tied to productivity, of not being enough as I am, and imposed it upon Cory to do more and work harder. And the truth is, I wasn't even aware of what I was doing until that moment after Dr. Brown's class. I was unaware of how my shame was coming out sideways, hurting the person I loved the most.

I know I'm not alone in this. Consider how we impose our own fears and needs for belonging and enoughness onto our friends and loved ones. Our "How will I . . ." questions become "How will *they* . . ." questions, particularly when the answers to those questions involve us.

How will I provide enough if I stop working eighty hours a week? Becomes *How will my partner provide enough if he stops working eighty hours a week?*

How will I get the promotion if I'm not doing extra work? Becomes *How will my mentee get the promotion if she's not doing the extra work?*

How will I be accepted if I were really honest about what I think or feel? Becomes *How will my kids be accepted if they are really honest about what they think or feel?*

See? We don't just strap our own feet to the accelerator and add weights to them, we also do the same to others. We pressure and shame others into moving at an unhealthy pace, leading them to believe they'll be more accepted, better off, and more successful if they do more or achieve more. And circling back to our understanding of precontemplation, we do all of this without fully realizing it.

Without awareness of the fear, anxiety, and pain attached to our accelerator, we will invariably project any of these unhealed fears, anxieties, and pains onto those around us, shaming them into adopting our own self-destructive behavior. Again, as Fr. Rohr says, whatever pain is not transformed will be transmitted.[8]

Numbing Through the Sacred

In May 2017, I stood before a room full of friends and strangers ready to confess my addiction. The spring semester of Oliver's arrival in 2016 woke me up to my addiction to hurry and hustling, and that summer offered the opportunity to begin confronting it.

A dear friend was launching a Twelve Step recovery ministry in January 2017, and our church group agreed to try out the curriculum the summer before its launch. But come January, when the ministry launched, I decided to jump in with both feet, help out, and dive further into my own recovery work.

It was a great opportunity to connect with friends each week, serve the church, and add a line on my résumé for community service (oh, how slippery our motivations can be as helpers). God moved fast through this decision, cutting through my mixed motives. Through studying the Twelve Steps of recovery, God showed me how I used productivity and speed to numb the pain from my childhood and the fear of not being enough. I heard the Divine whisper—*It's time to slow down*—and as I began to listen, I knew it was time to share with the rest of the group.

In the corner of a quiet room in the church, I read a carefully typed testimony to the group:

> Hi. My name is Holly. I'm recovering from perfectionism, overachievement, people-pleasing, and hustling for worthiness, accolades, and affirmations. I also admit to using various tactics, such as checking the news, email, and social media for superficial connection, to numb out, and to remove myself from the present moment.

As vulnerable as I felt saying those few sentences, it was the next one that shook me. My heart was pounding. My palms were sweaty. My throat was nearly closed shut to hold back the words I was about to say. Before I began to speak, tears were welling in my eyes. "My accelerator has been stuck for so long, *I don't know how to slow down*," I said shakily. My pride shattered in that moment.

That evening, I confessed that I was addicted to hustling and hurrying at an unsustainable pace. I was using the pace to mute the existential questions—*Do I belong? Am I worthy? Am I enough? Am I loved?*—but it wasn't helping. In fact, this pace was hurting those around me. It was stealing time from my family. It directed my attention to less important things. It left me distractable, stressed, and anxious.

The next month, I was invited back to speak on perfectionism, which was a corollary to my overfunctioning and overworking. I explained how my perfectionism presented. It wasn't about my house looking picture-perfect or my kids acting perfectly but rather was tied to a need to control and anticipate what's ahead in order to avoid pain. (Perfectionism is another tactic that keeps me quite busy.)

I shared how the gift of my 2016 maternity leave allowed me to read and journal and face some of the hard questions like *What am I doing to check out? How is my accelerator broken? When I choose work because it's easy over time with my family, who suffers?* (Spoiler: We all do.) The most difficult question, though, was gut-wrenching. *What will happen if my children are raised in a home where they perceive me as valuing accomplishments over presence?*

I also shared with this group that I'd begun to realize affirmations, accolades, successes, achievements, or perfections are idols our culture glorifies, that we get one sacred precious life, and that *this life is a gift*. As difficult as it was to navigate, I explained that my priorities had very slowly begun to shift from others' opinions of me or my résumé (or how clean my home is or how much I sacrifice myself for others) to how others experience me, how well I love them, and how they see me love others. I also explained the transformative role disciplined habits had in my life, many of which I'll share in the chapters ahead. These included replacing mindless activities with mindful practices that didn't have an agenda, motive, or possibility for an accolade to pop up. Instead, I was carving out the space I needed to be still, rest, play, and enjoy the gift of this life. It was this slower pace that energized me for the work I'd been called to do as a professor and researcher. And it was this slower pace that also supported me to be more present with my closest loved ones as a partner, mother, and friend.

The testimony ended with this prayer: "My hope and prayer are that each of you find some time to rest this week, whether it's five minutes or an entire day. We need the rest. We need presence over perfection. Because it's in the rest and the stillness that we find that still, small voice of God."

I shook almost the entire time as I read, which was unusual for me. As a professor, I've had a lot of public speaking practice. But reading these words to this group, some of whom I didn't know (with *zero control* over how they'd take my confession), unlocked something within me. I felt empowered to take another step toward a life grounded in my two core values of love and integrity.

I was bringing the honest layers of who I was into the light, layers that I had tried to separate and dis-integrate from my core identity to maintain the pace needed to hustle for and prove my worth. In openly sharing these honest reflections within a safe space, I was gently weaving these layers back into who I am and allowing a necessary healing to unfold through love and integration.

To be abundantly clear, this community had already begun to earn my trust and felt safe, allowing me to be this honest when I was asked to speak. My husband and some of my closest friends were in this group, but even among those I didn't know well, there was a shared understanding. Honesty, nonjudgmental compassion, and honoring others' (and our own) stories with safety and trust were core values within this community. They were the prerequisites to vulnerability and transformation.

Thank God for this space of safety and trust that allowed each of us to remove our armor for a couple of hours a week, to honor one another's stories and courage, to set down our dis-integrated layers of identity, to humbly learn from others' journeys, and to allow transformation to occur within ourselves and one another. In this nonjudgmental space with fellow travelers, I was able to remove the layers of armor I had habitually and addictively carried so that I could actually slow down.

Actually Slowing Down

Once you recognize the ways you use speed to keep the existential questions out of sight and out of mind, the next step is to take your foot off the accelerator. It is both as simple and as excruciatingly hard as that. But learning to slow down and living at a slow(er) pace is necessary if we're ever going to invite the Divine in. Put another way, we won't have time to recognize—much less sit with—our own existential questions if we keep hustling and hurrying from one thing to the next.

So how do we even slow down, especially when we've mostly done nothing but speed up for as long as we can remember? Consider a manual transmission car. As you shift down in gear, the car slows. (This is a thing I've been told time and time again, though I've never really learned how to drive a standard.) Then apply the same principle to your own life.

Consider the number of the hours you work, including hours spent on unpaid work. (Let's start with a hypothetical 60 hours.) Now, imagine taking your foot off the accelerator. Watch as your speed begins to slow. When you're ready, shift down from fifth gear to fourth, and notice how your speed slows. (Perhaps you move from 60 hours to 55 hours.) Stay in fourth gear as long as you need in order to notice a difference and get comfortable. Once you're comfortable at the slower pace, shift down again, this time to third gear (perhaps shifting from 55 hours to 50 hours). Notice what's happening internally as you slow down, how your body might resist the change in pace. Then shift down to second (perhaps shifting from 50 hours to 45 hours). Again, pause and get comfortable with the feeling. See how your body begs you to put your foot on the accelerator and upshift, stretching back toward that 100 mile-per-hour mark. Still, if you stay in second gear and allow space to open up, you might find time to look at those deeper questions, the questions of enoughness you've been trying to avoid. Finally, shift down to first gear (shifting from 45 hours to 40 hours).

In first gear, you're essentially coasting. And now, you have an additional 20 hours per week to face all those questions and to invite God to provide meaningful answers. Stay in that space. Coast a bit.

As uncomfortable as we may feel downshifting and learning to live at a slow(er) pace, this process is necessary to create space and allow the Divine to answer the existential questions around the inner pain we've avoided. This slowing down helps us begin to see the Sacred within instead of the blur of your life speeding by.

Now that you've slowed, the temptation to ramp your speed back up will surely come. How will you resist the temptation, especially after hurrying and hustling for so long? You'll need supports along the way. You'll need others to help steady you.

Reflection Exercises

In the last chapter, you identified pressures or fears that keep your foot attached to the accelerator. After reading this chapter, have they changed or are there others to add? To the best of your ability, identify any unhealthy coping mechanisms you use to avoid these anxieties, pressures, or fears.

Take a moment to look at your calendar over the last day, last week, last month, last quarter, and maybe the last year. Pay attention to any rhythms you find—are there regular seasons or times of the day when you find yourself tempted to hurry or hustle more? Reflect on the root of those temptations to hurry or hustle around those times—again, nonjudgmentally observe them simply to become more aware of them. At the same time, notice if there are seasons or days you find yourself content and comfortable with a slower pace, and, again, nonjudgmentally observe the root of that contentment and comfort.

Reflect on the downshifting practice. Think about a time you drove on a highway for a long period of time at 75 mph, and then got off at an exit, quickly shifting down to a 35 mph road. Do you remember that feeling in your body of wanting to go faster, the discomfort or discontentment with the slower speed after traveling so fast for so long? How does that translate to your speed of hustling and hurrying in all you do as a helper?

CHAPTER 6

Steady

*You are worth the quiet moment. You are worth the
deeper breath. You are worth the time it takes to
slow down, be still, and rest.*[1]

—Morgan Harper Nichols

Sir Isaac Newton, the famed English scientist, developed three laws
of motion, which are as follows:[2]

Law 1:   An object at rest will stay at rest, and an object in
motion will stay in motion with the same speed and
in the same direction unless a force acts upon it.

Law 2:   Force equals mass times acceleration. The bigger the
object and the more acceleration, the more force.

Law 3:   For every action, there is an equal and opposite reaction. Put another way, when you fire the cannon, the
explosion causes the ball to fly forward and the cannon to kick back.

Though Newton meant these laws to apply to the physical
world, they also seem to apply to our spirit and state of *being*, especially the first law. When we've been in motion for so long, we may
hit a wall (via burnout or sickness), and our bodies might stop. Still,
there's a momentum deep within, and we long to keep moving.
It's the same momentum that kept me going even after landing
facedown on our living room floor when Callie was an infant,

overwhelmed because the pace of life felt so unsustainable. It's the momentum I still feel and often give in to if I'm not paying careful attention. You might feel that same momentum in your body, mind, or heart too.

As we become aware of our momentum, we want to *work hard* to *achieve* a slower internal momentum speed. But that's not the way it works. What we need is a deep, transformative, healing process, and that takes time and patience.

So we must honestly recognize our internal, humming momentum, accept it for what it is, and let it teach us. We need to trust that we relied on that momentum to serve us for some reason for a particular time, while still questioning why we let it take over. We must recognize that this will not be a quick fix.

Most importantly, if we're going to solve our momentum dilemma, we will have to turn to Newton's third law—that for every action, there is an equal and opposite reaction. As we exploded out like a cannonball at terminal velocity, something was pushed back. Perhaps something like patience, surrender, or discernment. We need to return our attention to those virtues and practices we left in the rearview mirror as we pushed our foot on the accelerator.

Tuning In: Practicing Scanning the Body, Heart, and Mind

Before we explore supports that help us find a sense of steadiness in maintaining our slower pace, let's practice tuning in to our inner landscapes. In fact, I would encourage you to lean on this practice throughout the book as sensations, feelings, and thoughts surface.

Take a moment to pause, close your eyes, and breathe. Do you notice it? The sensational hum in your muscles, ready to go, do, and serve. Maybe you feel like a machine that's been charged and stuck in go, go, go. Even this brief moment of slower contemplation may feel unnatural, and yet you know deep within that you're not a machine but a human being.

Sit with this sensation for a moment and nonjudgmentally observe it. Don't try to fix it, but simply notice it. Now take another deep breath, filling your belly with air (engaging in diaphragmatic breathing).[3] Breathe out, and as you exhale, let the sensation you noticed go.

Continue breathing and turn your attention to your heart. Do you feel it? An ache or longing for a sense of love, safety, and rest? Maybe you've been so desperate for this love, safety, and rest that you cannot help but instinctively hustle for them through all that doing. Even in this moment, your tender and tired heart is uncertain of how to feel that love, safety, and rest after years of hustling for them, and yet, you know deep within that you're worth that inner peace.

Sit with this feeling for a moment and nonjudgmentally observe it. Don't try to fix it, but simply notice it. Take another deep breath, filling your belly with air, and as you exhale, let the feeling go.

Continue breathing and turn your attention to your mind. Do you hear it, that inner voice that questions your worth? The one that fills you with imposter syndrome even though you know you're inherently beloved? Does it seem as though your mind has oscillated between knowing your inherent worth and battling your inner critic? Have you been listening to the louder, outside voices for so long that it's difficult to discern the still, small voice within?

Sit with this thought for a moment and nonjudgmentally observe it. Don't try to fix it, but simply notice it. Take another deep breath, filling your belly with air, and as you exhale, let this thought go.

Now pause. As someone who is well acquainted with the temptation to hurry on to the next section in order to finish the book and move on to the next one, I hope you're able to sit with what surfaced in your body, heart, and mind for a moment, breathe, and be. Perhaps the guide above resonates or perhaps you simply consider the following questions:

What sensations do I notice when I scan my body?

What emotions do I notice when I tune into my heart?

What thoughts do I notice when I quiet my mind?

Throughout this journey of seeking the Sacred, return to these three questions as often as you need. As you begin practicing the supports listed in this chapter to steady yourself with a slower pace, these questions will help you remain mindful of that humming momentum beneath everything, including your temptations to jump back to a state of speed.

Start with Your *Why* and Identify Structures to Help Find a Sense of Steady

As much as we'd like to "hurry up and slow down," we need new skills, tools, and supports to steady ourselves as we adjust to our new, slower pace of being. First among those tools is to define our *why*.[4] Why are we choosing to slow down, particularly when it cuts against the grain of our culture, comfort, and even occupational norms?

Is it because I'm burning out and don't have time, energy, or attention to be the helper I want to be?

Is it because I don't have time to be present to the Divine in the moment or in myself, much less in others?

Is it because a part of me, deep within, just knows this isn't the pace at which I was designed to operate?

Once you clarify your *why*, it's time to explore what supports you'll need to keep you steady as you follow this slower pace. For me, these include receiving help from others, tuning in and supporting my body, practicing Sabbath, structuring social media usage, finding the courage to create and hold boundaries, practicing patience, and embracing curiosity and surrender whenever I want to speed up. For what it's worth, I often still find myself fighting against these supports. Similar to the pre-nap meltdown of a toddler—*I don't want to take a nap!*—I've pushed hard against these supports, even knowing they're good for me. Over time, though, I've come to understand just how much they helped sustain a slower pace and thus my ability to connect with the Divine, motivating me to continue practicing them.

We're all uniquely created with different needs, resources, and abilities. What worked for me might not work for you. Still, let's look at the steadying supports that have helped me most.

Receiving Support from Others

Even after admitting my struggle with slowing down in that recovery group, it took time to slow down, especially with the demands of a busy life. By September 2017, I was beginning an administrative position I was honored to step into, despite lacking the confidence that I could do the job. Plus, I was still on the tenure track, involved in about four research projects, writing several academic articles, mentoring students, participating in committees, traveling for conferences, and teaching too many classes. I was also about a year and a half into being a mom of two very different but equally loved children. By the end of the spring 2018 semester, still having not slowed down despite my confession (but having sped up to meet the growing demands), I had reached a level of burnout I'd honestly never experienced before.

I finally realized I couldn't slow down on my own. I needed help. I needed structures, scaffolding, and social support to steady me as I eased off the gas. With no idea what to do, I scheduled an appointment with my doctor to talk about burnout. Later that day, I sat in the doctor's office with Cory, who had graciously agreed to come with me because I wanted him to hear whatever the doctor might say.

When my doctor came into the room, I was nearly in tears explaining that I was drowning from the sense of overwhelm. And though I taught my students coping skills to deal with these kinds of feelings, I was completely unable to use them myself. In fact, I confessed that I actually felt *guilty* for being in his office.

Didn't my doctor have other patients with more pressing needs?

Who was I to be crying and asking for help in the midst of having a great job, healthy family, access to clean water and food, a house, and sense of safety?

My inner critic was fierce and relentless that day. And though I assumed my doctor would listen and prescribe me an antidepressant to help me break through the fog—recognizing that medication can a be necessary gift—he took a different approach.[5]

He began asking me questions about what I enjoy, things I'm doing when I feel well, whether I hold boundaries, and what I'd do more of if I had the time. As I responded, Cory (being the good partner that he is) occasionally jumped in to clarify when I minimized things. Then my doctor asked me what got in the way of those things.

Where to start?

I admitted my inability to say no to others, how I was drowning in email and felt the need to immediately respond to each, and how I constantly checked my phone and social media. I ate on the go too often, drank too many cups of coffee to get me going and too many glasses of wine to wind me down. I woke up early *and* stayed up late to work. All of it left me feeling disconnected from my husband, kids, myself, and God. He listened with such tender curiosity and care, echoing what I knew to be true: things needed to change, or my health and relationships would severely suffer.

After those ten minutes of finally opening up about these struggles, my doctor scribbled down his prescription. It included twelve simple steps.

1. Say "no" once weekly.
2. Shut my email dinger off and hide the number of emails in my inbox.
3. Allow a predetermined amount of time for email daily.
4. Prioritize responses to email by importance.
5. Spend ten minutes outside twice daily.
6. Walk in the office and spend time in prayer.
7. Exercise three times per week.
8. Eat clean (minimally processed foods) at least once daily.
9. Read to the kids three nights per week.
10. Have a weekly date night.
11. Set a nightly bedtime.
12. Limit email time at home and put my phone away at a set time.

After writing out the prescription, he added three x's for signatures: mine, Cory's, and his. I brought the makeshift contract home and hung it on the refrigerator, where it has stayed ever since.

Accountability—from our partner, friends, and even doctors—is a powerful tool for steadying our pace. Cory and my doctor were my first two accountability partners. My therapist, spiritual director, family, and recovery community also provided support and accountability. Even at work, I began asking colleagues for accountability with my pace. With the support of my dean, I stepped down as chair of one committee, let someone else teach a class, and asked my graduate assistants to take on more responsibility. And with all this support, it became easier to practice saying no (even *weekly!*), limiting my email time, and turning work off.

I couldn't hold that sort of weight and transition without the help and accountability from others I trusted. And in that new rhythm, I could confront the fear that I was not enough and continue the process of healing.

Supporting Your Body

As I continued to slow down, I invited my therapist into the journey. And though I was paying closer attention to my thoughts and emotions, I was less aware of my body. During our sessions, as we discussed my process of slowing down, my therapist asked where I felt different emotions in my body. I was at a loss.

Growing up, I rarely heard messages about my body being good or worth my attention. So when it tried to tell me it was tired, hungry, or needed to move, I ignored its pleas, seeing them as inconveniences getting in the way of the work I "needed" to do. Yet, when shame washed over me, when the feeling of not being enough set in, just before my people-pleasing and hustling tendencies kicked in, my body responded. My throat tightened. My palms sweat. I'd have vertigo, a knotted stomach, and a feeling of thick, heavy armor falling into place around my chest. Still, before talking with my therapist and reading a well-timed book on the issue, I couldn't have named any of those things. I was so unaware that my nervous system was in a state of perpetual panic to get me to safety.

In therapist Aundi Kolber's book *Try Softer*, she invites the reader to push against the socially celebrated message to "try harder."[6] In her book, which is packed with tools that help us learn to not press so hard, Aundi showed me how to recognize my own autonomic nervous system's response to the trauma I'd experienced as a child. She helped me understand the fawn response—a lesser-known stress response alongside fight, flight, or freeze that deeply resonated.[7] In response to any danger, overwhelm, or threats in social situations, I turned to people-pleasing, especially when the risk of rejection was high. This people-pleasing led me to say yes to everything and to consistently do more for others (beyond my capacity), which naturally increased the pace of my life. It's the coping mechanism I can trace back the furthest into childhood.

As I better understood that my body was automatically responding to present situations based on my childhood trauma, it was like I was suddenly off the hook. My body had adapted and been wired to constantly focus on others' needs and preferences to protect itself from rejection and abuse. This didn't mean I didn't have to change—I did. But it meant there were instinctive responses to stressors and risks of rejection that were beyond my awareness or control. This created an invitation to be softer with myself.

Attention to our body is critical in the process of steadying our balance after slowing down. Aundi writes that,

> Trying softer allows us to recognize that we must figure out how to establish safety for our bodies. If we can listen to and respond to our bodies' needs, whether that means releasing energy by getting outside or staying connected to ourselves through conscious breathing, our window of tolerance will begin to grow, and true healing can occur. It is slow work, but friend, nothing could be more worth it.[8]

I wholeheartedly agree.

For years, I'd carried pain in my shoulders, neck, and chest when I was trying harder. I couldn't understand what my body was telling me. And so, I grew angry with my body instead of simply asking, *What are you trying to show me?* But in the last few years, I've practiced paying attention to and being kinder with my body. More often than not, when a new pain arises, it's trying to tell me something very specific: "You're carrying too much, doing too much, too stressed out, trying too hard to prove you're enough."

As you learn to listen to your body, check in with your own pain points. Ask what your body is trying to show you and wait for an answer. Consider a few examples.

> *Shoulders, why do you hurt so much?* Maybe it's because they're carrying a lot more weight and stress than you were made to carry.
>
> *Chest, why do you feel so tight?* Maybe your shoulders have been hunched over to guard your heart as you run from meeting to meeting.
>
> *Neck and head, why do you both hurt so badly?* Maybe they're counterbalancing the heavy weight you've been carrying as you push forward and do more.
>
> *Oh, dear body, why do you feel so exhausted?* Maybe it's because you shaved off an hour of sleep the last few nights to meet that deadline.

Once you identify what your body is trying to tell you, express gratitude. Do your best to better care for your body going forward. In fact, consider writing a letter like I did in January 2020 before my research leave to work on this book:[9]

> *Dear body, I am so sorry I've ignored you for so long. I neglected you as you continued to care for and protect me throughout my life, while following along with my ego's need to push harder. Like a wise mentor, you were*

trying to communicate with me, trying to signal the warn-
ing signs, trying to invite me to slow down and care for
us, and I missed all of the "check engine" lights. We were
burning out and I'm so sorry I didn't listen. I'm listening.
Thank you for doing the best you could with my stubborn-
ness and addiction to trying harder for so long. Please for-
give me.

Sabbath: A Support for Your Soul

Before I ask this question, take a deep breath. Now, fellow helper, when was the last time you took a day of rest? A full, unscheduled, do-as-you-please, playful, soul-at-peace, unproductive day of rest? Or, if a full day of rest isn't possible, when's the last time you took a morning or afternoon to go outside for a wandering walk, to purposelessly play or create, or to snuggle up with a cup of tea and a novel? When's the last time you gave your soul permission to stop striving and simply be?

The notion of Sabbath comes from the Jewish tradition and commemorates the seventh day of the week, the day God rested from creation work. It originates from the fourth of the Ten Commandments to reserve the seventh day as holy and for rest. And though traditional Jews still recognize the Sabbath (or Shabbat) on Saturday, many Christians observe Sunday as their Sabbath. Similarly, several other religious traditions, and even some who are not religious, observe a day of rest too.

The topic of taking a rest day has long been a shame minefield for me. During graduate school, colleagues and professors pleasantly asked about one another's weekends, and the default answer was, "Whew! I got *so much* work done!" which was immediately celebrated. Never did I hear anyone push back, encouraging the other to take a break. Never did I hear a professor say, "How was your Sabbath?"

Naturally, I fell right in line. I adopted the approach to weekend work for three reasons. First, it was the predominant cultural message. Second, affirmation can be an addictive drug and overworking was certainly affirmed. Third, and practically speaking, Cory and I were flat broke in graduate school, and I was determined to finish my PhD as quickly as possible to avoid more student loan debt and to make more than $1,100 a month for my research assistantship.

When you spend weekend after weekend working, catching up, completing tasks, and planning for the upcoming week, do you know what's lost? Rest. Recovery. Creativity. Play. Time and memories with loved ones. Life. And most importantly, space to experience the Divine in and around you.

In graduate school, I began practicing Sabbath slowly. Callie and I would go to church together on Sunday morning and afterward, we'd visit Cory during his shift at a local coffee shop. As she napped after lunch, I curled up on the couch with my journal for an hour. I protected that Sunday routine, and when Cory came home and Callie woke up, I shifted back into work mode to focus on my dissertation. Still, the time at church followed by a few hours with zero connection to work or email was my life raft during that season of life.

Slowly, I've stretched those few hours to an entire day. Of course, there are times when we may need to work more, when we have to spend a few hours catching up over the weekend. So, I'm sensitive to the ebb and flow of this practice. But I try to resist celebrating a student who regularly works all weekend, and instead, ask how I can help or support them in stopping the unsustainable pattern of behavior.

Consistent Sabbath rest is one of the primary structures I use today to ensure my pace stays balanced. But maybe you don't know how to practice this kind of rest. Start by setting aside one day a week with no time spent on work. Don't catch up on emails or do anything tied to your job. Do it for one month, then reflect upon how you feel. If you need more helpful tips, I recommend Dr. Saundra Dalton-Smith's *Sacred Rest*.[10] It is a valuable guide to the seven different kinds of rest we need (physical, mental, emotional, spiritual, social, sensory, and creative), why we need rest, and how to attain more of it.

Structuring Social Media Usage

One of the topics I mentioned wrestling with during those recovery meetings was my addiction to social media and my phone. Email, Facebook, and Instagram all served as meaningful ways to personally and professionally connect with others. Still, these apps split my focus, sped up my hustling tactics, and sucked me into endless loops of notifications. But if they were meaningful tools, why did I feel so addicted?

In my season of learning to slow down, I began to get curious about these forms of technology that drew me toward constant engagement and checking. As I fought to understand why I couldn't just put my phone down and stop thinking about it, I picked up Dr. Adam Alter's book *Irresistible: The Rise of Addictive Technology and the Business of Keeping Us Hooked*, which offered a massive wake-up call.[11] Through his research, he demonstrated how brilliant engineers, marketers, and psychologists have designed these apps to be addictive. They use science to strategically and *constantly* keep us stuck in the apps.

I love the connections and opportunities social media and email can provide. I also love learning from others and have had the privilege of meeting in real life many whom I've connected with in virtual spaces. At the same time, my phone was a growing distractor, keeping me busy, and constantly stealing my attention from the present moment. Even if I wasn't on a social media app, I'd catch myself thinking about checking it. Through reading *Irresistible*, I realized that email and social media contributed to my hustling and hurrying during stressful seasons when I was most vulnerable to fears of worthlessness.

So, what did I do? Knowing I needed to cut the apps most guilty of taking my time and attention, I deactivated my social media accounts and took email off my phone for *long* stretches of time—between six months and a year—a few times. Why did I do this? After years of being on social media, I needed to detox and know what it was like to exist without constantly being available to others through a device. I needed to reserve my limited energy, time, and attention to focus on slowing down and healing. And I needed to relearn how to remain deeply present with my closest loved ones without thinking about a post or whether comments were waiting to be checked. Simply put, I didn't need my device to be yet another thing pressuring me into constantly hustling, and I was resentful of the ways it's designed to be addictive.

Unplugging from social media helped me to remember that I cannot be everything for everyone all of the time. Even my online engagement had the potential of becoming a form of people-pleasing and performing to achieve self-worth. Unplugging also helped me admit I am just as vulnerable as anyone to social media's design to be addictive. After all, brilliant software engineers and developers designed these apps to manipulate me, rewire my brain to crave the dopamine bumps those notifications offer, and to lure me into hustling for affection on their platforms.[12] In placing structures and boundaries around my social media use these days, what have I found as a result? My attention span to my inner landscape exponentially grows when it isn't stretched so thin by certain forms of technology.

Boundaries, Courage, and Patience

Maintaining boundaries is one of the hardest things for many of us as helpers, myself included.[13] This is why my doctor's prescription included the directive to say "no" at least once weekly. (He actually first wrote daily and changed to weekly when he saw the look on my face.) I genuinely try to set boundaries, usually at the beginning of the semester, always with eager hope and determination. Within days, requests and opportunities come in, and my carefully curated boundaries begin to evaporate if I don't fight to maintain them.

The *practice* of creating boundaries is worth it, even though they don't always hold. Why is this practice worth it? Because creating and holding boundaries are a sort of mental health practice that involves humility, requiring you to recognize your limitations. We simply cannot do everything for everyone. And even when I must modify (or transgress) my boundaries, they're at least there to remind me of my limitations. The boundaries become a place to check in and ask, "Do I have the time or energy for this new opportunity? Is it worth the stress?"

Creating and holding those boundaries requires courage. People will not love your boundaries, especially when you've trained others to ignore them. Still, your boundaries protect you from burnout, and those closest to you will thank you for maintaining them. In fact, consider inviting your loved ones into your boundary-setting process for accountability.

Creating boundaries will also be uncomfortable at first. Just as new physical exercises or yoga poses cause muscles we haven't used in a while to ache, we might ache a little as we uphold our boundaries. Still, each time you feel that twinge of pain when you say no, trust that the discomfort is temporary. And as you stretch and settle into your boundaries, notice that you're making space to recognize the Sacred within yourself.

Structured Curiosity and Surrender

In order to navigate the journey of seeking the Sacred—first in ourselves and then in others—curiosity is a nonnegotiable. In fact, it's a key ingredient to psychological flexibility, or our mind's ability to be agile and adaptable. Along this journey of seeking the Sacred, curiosity allows us to gently ask why we felt the need to hustle for so long.

Acceptance and commitment therapy (ACT) is one way to help us gain psychological flexibility.[14] This therapeutic approach helps us nonjudgmentally view and accept our thoughts and emotions, while ensuring our behaviors align with our core values and goals. During our sessions, my therapist (who's trained in ACT) helps me get curious about moments when I'm showing a tendency toward speeding up, indicating a move away from my values and goals.

Moving at a slower pace, I have more time and energy to get curious with each opportunity, and if I feel drawn to accept it, I ask why. This curiosity keeps me from reacting as quickly as I once had and helps me to better discern when and how to respond. Through this kind of grounded curiosity, the need to hustle has, for the most part, loosened its grip on my life.

As I've practiced curiosity with my therapist, I've noticed the practice of surrender surface. It doesn't feel like giving up, but rather, setting down the ways I've idolized the illusion of control that keep me hustling for more. Interestingly, curiosity teaches me to surrender to the present moment, to do what is mine to do, and to trust it is enough *and* that I am enough. Through this work, the need to hustle is loosening its grip even more.

Seeing the Steadying Structures
Come Together

Adopting each of these structures took time. When I lose sight of them—and I do from time to time when the pressure mounts—I have to mindfully return. I have to seek out accountability, listen to my body, honor Sabbath, turn off social media, reset my boundaries, and carve out time to get curious about my pace. Although the practices don't offer immediate results, with diligence, over time, they help.

After putting these supportive structures in place, I began to see how they work together to create space for holy moments, for seeing the Sacred in me and in the world around me. But one morning in the summer of 2018, I realized they really were working.

When Callie and Oliver wake up each day, they shuffle into my home office to say good morning, give me a big hug, and connect for a few moments. Afterward, they generally return to the kitchen to make breakfast with Cory while I finish writing before coming out to spend a little time with them.

One morning, Callie seemed to have about 500 reasons to keep coming back into my office and interrupt my writing. When I heard her approach my office door for the 501st time, I felt the urge to snap. Instead, I paused, took a very deep breath, flipped my palms up, and asked God to please give me patience. I surrendered to God in that moment, despite every fiber within me wanting to immediately send her back out. I slowly turned to her and gently said, "Hey, sweetie, what do you need?"

"Here you go, Mommy!" she said with a radiant smile, extending a piece of paper that had "today's to do's" printed across the top. On it, she traced her hand, drew a heart in the middle of her palm, and scribbled in her wobbly five-year-old handwriting, "You are the best mommy ever." Instantly, my heart tugged in every direction and hot tears streamed down my face as I fully felt the weight of that holy moment.

I had been milliseconds away from reacting by telling her to go away. And all she wanted was to share her art and her love with me. If I had told her to go away, what would she have thought looking at the picture she drew and words she wrote? Would I have ever seen the picture, or would she have trashed it in a moment of heartache? With wet cheeks, I hugged her, thanked her for this precious gift, *received her love*, hung up the picture, and sat with the holy lesson. By surrendering and making space to be fully present, I'd allowed the Sacred in Callie to reach out to the Sacred in me.

The picture that Callie drew hangs in my office as a reminder that when we slow down, when we incorporate structures to help us maintain the speed our soul needs, we make space for sacred moments. Those sacred moments remind us of what's most important. They steady us. And it's a lesson that's so important to me that, shortly after that event, I visited a local tattoo artist and had Callie's little heart from that drawing tattooed onto the inside of both of my wrists. Now when my palms are facing up, I see them. Those hearts remind me to live with a posture of open palms and to surrender so that I may operate at a slow enough pace to see the Sacred in each moment and receive the messages that I am loved.

The steadying structures held me in a slower pace and allowed me to experience moments of Sacred interaction. They continued to support me along this journey of seeking the Sacred within myself and in those around me, particularly as I moved into the next, perhaps most difficult stage—Stillness.

Reflection Exercises

Practice listening to your body. What sensations do you notice when you scan your body? What emotions do you notice when you tune into your heart? What thoughts do you notice when you quiet your mind? What is your body trying to tell you?

Identify one or two people that you can practice receiving support from this week, such as your partner or a friend. If they offer help, can you practice accepting it? Or can you think of one thing they can do to help you and practice vulnerably asking for that help? (It could be as simple as reminding you to go to bed by a certain time or picking up an order from the store.)

Which (if any) of the practices in this chapter seems easiest to incorporate into your life as a structure to help you maintain a slower pace? Why? Which (if any) of these practices seem the most difficult and why? What supports are needed for you to try these practices as you find your sense of steadiness?

CHAPTER 7

Still

Be still, and know that I am God.

—Psalm 46:10 (NIV)

Before my parents' divorce, we lived in a house that sat on the edge of Lake Ontario in upstate New York. As a kid, I looked out my bedroom window and saw a seemingly endless body of water. I watched waterspouts dance above the waves during storms as lightning flashed above. In the winter, I walked along the icy shore and saw water burst up through the top of ice volcanoes with each wave. I sat on the dock, fished at sunset, and watched the sun go down over Irondequoit. At night, I marveled at the stars and looked for satellites while listening to the waves. Sometimes I took out the canoe for a morning adventure. I often found my sanctuary on the rocky shore as I breathed in the lake air.

In the most difficult times of my youth, I'd sit in our backyard and look over the lake. There, I found myself distracted from my physical, psychological, and emotional wounds. I watched for patterns in the waves, contemplatively following the caps until they broke on the shore. If I couldn't go outside, I sat at the edge of my bed and cranked the screenless windows open. I listened to the waves and birds, smelled the lake air, and noticed the water's surface. When it was calm and the lake looked like glass, I felt calm. When the water was rough and the lake resembled my internal emotional state, I felt validated. I found a sense of safety and security in this lake, which offered me a sanctuary to identify and regulate my many emotions as someone who feels emotions deeply, especially in the midst of facing so many layers of pain.

I often think of the lake and its parallels with life. When the wind whipped the waves up, or when the lake "turned over" in the fall, I couldn't see past the surface. It was too choppy or muddy. But on many summer mornings, when the lake was as smooth as glass with a layer of haze on the water, I took our canoe to paddle out in solitude and find peace and stillness within myself as I embraced the peace and stillness around me. In that peace, I looked over the side of the canoe and saw the bottom of the lake, even far offshore. I saw the rocks at the bottom, some aquatic plants waving, a school of minnows darting, and the sun's light dancing on the bottom of the lake.

In the stillness, I could see.

I don't live with a lake in my backyard anymore, but I still respond to bodies of water in the same way as when I was young. And I still see the parallel to my own inner space.

In stillness, I can see what's happening below the surface.

In stillness, I can rest and let things *be*, without needing to control them.

In stillness, I can reflect and see myself.

In stillness, I can receive peace, and ultimately, share the gift of that peace with others.

On the other hand, when I'm moving too fast (whether in a canoe or in my life) and I look over the edge to the water, I cannot see into the deep. The ripples and waves caused by my movement prevent me from seeing what's below.

When we aren't still, we can't *really* examine much past the distorted surface.

When we aren't still, we often make assumptions and decisions based on the distorted reflection of ourselves.

When we aren't still, we misinterpret or completely miss the accurate and authentic reality of what's inside.

We need stillness to truly examine our lives but being still is hard for many of us. How do we do it? Chapter 6 offered tangible practices to help create the structures and boundaries we need to steady our balance from slowing down. This chapter offers movements within those structures and boundaries to usher us toward inner stillness. But as we move into the work of stillness, understand there is an ebb and flow between each of the stages of seeking the Sacred. We're always moving in and out of the stages, always refining our speed, shoring up our steadying structures, and practicing stillness (along with the other stages).

Practices That Help Us Be with Stillness

Learning to be still is hard work, especially if you've never really practiced it. Many of us give into the current around us, which moves at a pace far too fast for our souls. We've contributed to that current by hurrying to keep up with it, often for as long as we can remember. But at some point, if we want to see a deeper reality, we must become still.

If we let it, stillness can become an act of resistance. Through stillness, we resist the systems that *want* us to operate at a speed that distracts us from contemplation and from what matters most, including our loved ones and our own souls. We resist the current that sweeps us away from the grounded, inherent belovedness God wants us to experience.

To participate in this resistance that stillness offers, we need contemplative practices to guide us. We need to engage in what Catholic priest, professor, and theologian Henri Nouwen called, "the discipline of the heart." In his 1988 book *Letters to Marc*, Nouwen examined the pace of modern life. He wrote,

It strikes me increasingly just how hard-pressed people are nowadays. It's as though they're tearing about from one emergency to another. Never solitary, never still, never really free but always busy about something that just can't wait. You get the impression that, amid this frantic hurly-burly, we lose touch with life itself. We have the experience of being busy while nothing real seems to happen. The more agitated we are, and the more compacted our lives become, the more difficult it is to keep a space where God can let something truly new really take place.

The discipline of the heart helps us to let God into our hearts so that God can become known to us there, in the deepest recesses of our own being.[1]

Nouwen saw that the pace of life often drags us away from seeing and knowing God. The discipline of the heart allows us to be still long enough to see and experience God in our lives.

It's this stillness that calms the inner waves that react to everything. In doing so, we begin to see that we cannot push into every storm. We can't help everyone in our lives with everything. We cannot take on every responsibility or opportunity. Stillness allows us to clearly see and discern how to respond with what's truly ours to do as helpers.

Nouwen writes of two other important disciplines: solitude and silence. Where solitude disconnects our need for others' approval so we can deeply connect with the Divine, silence quiets the mental chatter and outer messages so we can intimately hear and trust the still, small voice within.

Both solitude and silence dance with the practice of stillness, and I'll discuss them more in the next chapter. For now, let's focus on stillness. Stillness allows the space for us to hear from and interact with the Sacred inside us. What practices might support this kind of discipline of the heart? And how do we cultivate this stillness within, especially being surrounded by the fast and strong current around us? The practices below create space for stillness and have been some of the most transformative ones for me. My hope is that you'll consider exploring them more deeply, drawing on the ones that most align with your unique journey and needs.

Cultivating Stillness of the Heart Through Centering Prayer

Although various forms of meditation exist across faith traditions, many of which have been shown to support our well-being, one distinct practice within the Christian tradition has been my favorite—centering prayer.[2] This practice includes four main guidelines:

1. Choose a sacred word as the symbol of your intention to consent to God's presence and action within.
2. Sitting comfortably and with eyes closed, settle briefly and silently introduce the sacred word as the symbol of your consent to God's presence and action within.
3. When engaged with your thoughts [including body sensations, feelings, images, and reflections], return ever-so-gently to the sacred word.
4. At the end of the prayer period, remain in silence with eyes closed for a couple of minutes.[3]

Although there are seasons where my practice is more centered and consistent, I try to show up to my prayer chair most mornings, lean on my sacred word, return to my breath when distractions surface, and discover the centeredness eventually returns. What does this look like, practically speaking? To move this from a lofty idea to how this plays out, here's what a typical centering prayer session looks like for me, recognizing it may look different for each person.[4]

It's five thirty in the morning. I silence my alarm, roll out of bed, and quietly shuffle to the dark living room. I grab my phone, open the Insight Timer application, adjust the volume to 6 percent, and sit in my prayer chair. I read the day's Henri Nouwen passage in Gabrielle Earnshaw's *You Are the Beloved* and start the ten-second countdown on Insight Timer for twenty minutes of centering prayer. My palms flip up, my feet are on the ground, I sit up, and breathe.

dinggg

Breathe in through my nose. Breathe out through my mouth.

I release any sense of control, consent to God's presence and action within, and pray: *"Good morning, God. I give You my heart and surrender to Your will. Whatever You do within my heart during this time is none of my business."*

Breathe in through my nose. Breathe out through my mouth.

I keep my mouth open to avoid having to open and close it, moving my tongue to and away from the roof of my mouth to engage in diaphragmatic breathing. My sacred word is "rest," and I return to it when my mind wanders, which doesn't take long.

Work. That meeting, that colleague, that email.

Rest.

The manuscript, the podcast, the to-do list item.

(The war for my attention has begun.)

Breathe in through my nose. Breathe out through my mouth. Rest.

Within seconds, I'm thinking of my children, wishing I had read to them the night before, remembering it's crazy sock day at school, wondering about the soccer signup deadline. My arm itches.

Breathe in through my nose. Breathe out through my mouth. Rest.

I manage to quiet my mind, at least for a moment. Then, more thoughts: Cory and I haven't been on a date in months. The backyard is a mess. Our twelve-year-old dog, Lucy, is sick. Tears surface as I wonder how much longer she'll be with us.

Breathe in through my nose. Breathe out through my mouth. Rest.

My focus returns to my breath. I let go of everything else and consent to God's work within me, recognizing it's beyond my control. I drop my awareness from my thoughts to my innermost being and *practice* surrendering.

About ten to twelve minutes in, I finally rest. I feel the deep stillness, silence, and solitude. I'm at peace, alone in the dark with my family asleep, surrendered to a healing process that is beyond what I can control, create, or cause to happen. My ego wants to know what God's up to, but it has no idea. So I surrender, let go of controlling, knowing, predicting, or assuming. Instead, I rest in God's love and trust in God's care for me.

This is stillness.

This is how I begin most days, but it was *not* how I began my days before 2016. Even after I began practicing centering prayer, I only managed five minutes every few days, and I hoped for some divine intervention while my mind wandered. The truth is, I wasn't comfortable resting in God's care and it took years to sink into this rhythm. Still, something was changing within me, even in those brief sessions.

One morning in 2018, I saw the difference these sessions were making in my life. I had planned to go to my office for a podcast interview about Namaste Theory with my friend Steve, but I was running late. I hurried to my car, barely put together. Just as I pushed the button to unlock my door, I saw it—a flat tire.

The thoughts started racing: *What should I do? Should I cancel? What will Steve think? Cory's running errands so I can't use his car*— But midstream, the thoughts stopped. And without warning, I laughed. Out loud. A full-on belly laugh.

I looked up, smiled, and chuckled over God's humor. God had been whispering to slow down, but I wasn't exactly listening. However, because of those centering prayer practices, I could finally be still and notice God in the moment. I saw the flat tire for what it was—an invitation to practice slowing down, seeing the Divine, and surrendering to the present moment.

I took a picture and sent it to Cory, still laughing, and asked if he'd mind helping with it when he had time. *No rush*, I texted. And I meant it. I walked back inside and recorded the podcast episode from home with a deep peace.

It may have taken a year and a half of practicing centering prayer to notice any evidence, but something was changing within me. That was the first time I noticed it, and I haven't turned back since. Now I spend about twenty minutes in centering prayer each morning. It's sort of a daily vitamin for my soul. It strengthens my resolve to slow down and loosens my grip on the things I can't control. It helps me submit to a deep healing that I cannot do within myself. And in that stillness each morning, I am reminded of my identity as God's Beloved.

Centering prayer is my favorite practice for cultivating stillness, but it's not the only one. Truthfully, centering prayer alone wouldn't be enough to anchor me in stillness, stubborn as I am, and there are companion practices that go with it.

Stilling the Inner Critic—Nonjudgmental Self-Observation

Nonjudgmental self-observation allows us to examine our lives as they are without imposing judgments on our inner experiences. It's a meditation technique rooted in Buddhism and tied to mindfulness.[5] This practice is also regularly considered within the therapeutic intervention dialectical behavioral therapy (DBT).[6] Nonjudgmental self-observation is a supportive practice for both our mental health and spiritual journeys, allowing us to take note of distractions or stray thoughts and let them float on by without feeling shame. More importantly, it allows us to get curious about our initial inner sensations, thoughts, and feelings, and to separate ourselves enough to first observe rather than react to them. It's an important companion practice to centering prayer, and more importantly, it is necessary to fully see the Sacred within.

How do we practice nonjudgmental self-observation? Well, we briefly practiced a version of this in the last chapter under the "Tuning In" section as we identified a thought, feeling, or sensation within, and noticed it without needing to change it. The same principles apply in other spaces, including centering prayer. I offered a few examples of my "invitations to return to my breath" in the section above. But sometimes, I'll find that heavy, shipwreck-like thoughts, emotions, and sensations will surface in the midst of practicing centering prayer (perhaps memories from my childhood, new understandings around my ways of being, or some grief that I've instinctively repressed). Tears may fall as these thoughts, emotions, or sensations surface, but I nonjudgmentally observe them, giving them the space to exist even as I continue breathing.

Giving the thoughts, emotions, or sensations space is not enough, though. Nonjudgmental self-observation requires us to pause, breathe, and get curious about those things that have come to our awareness. Name the emotions. Do you feel sadness (or loneliness, apathy) or anger (or envy, grief)? Maybe you're full of joy or peace or love. Or maybe it's a sensation—your jaw tightens or shoulders relax. Notice and get curious about these, without jumping to fix them.

Nonjudgmental self-observation not only allows us to observe what's happening within, but it also allows us to learn from what's within. And what better time to *practice* nonjudgmental self-observation than during centering prayer, when distractions come rushing into our consciousness? Hopefully in these safer, calmer moments, it's less likely that our trauma responses are activated, allowing us more energy and attention to focus on the practice.

Still, there are other moments in our active lives to engage in nonjudgmental self-observation. When we get the promotion, our kids come home from college, a family member makes a cutting remark, or we receive an acceptance letter—we can pause, breathe, and become curious about the thoughts, emotions, and sensations bubbling up. Rather than getting swept away with them, we can step back and observe without judgment, refraining from attaching words like *good* or *bad* to our thoughts, emotions, or sensations. And if those thoughts, emotions, or sensations stick with us, we can carry them into our centering prayer the following day and offer them to God.

Like centering prayer, we need to practice nonjudgmental self-observation often. Consider hanging a sign in your home that reminds you to still yourself from time to time and take note of your internal landscape without judgment. These reminders and regular practices may serve you well during those unexpected highs and lows of life—particularly the highs and lows of being a helper—as you learn to take the time to curiously observe before reacting. What will you find in that space between observation and reaction? If your experience is anything like mine, you'll find a divine opportunity to hear from the Sacred within to discern your next step.

The "Be Still" Prayer

After high school, I spent one semester at St. Bonaventure University, where I joined a small student group that met with two Franciscans—Brother Joe and Father Dan—on Sunday evenings.[7] In a small room within the campus ministry center, the two led us through a weekly meditation and prayer service. This group became my church and place of belonging, separate from the thrill-seeking behaviors, struggles with depression, and hopes of fitting in during my first semester of college.

Each week we gathered, took some deep breaths, and began reciting the "Be Still" prayer based on Psalm 46:10, which moved us to a restful state of *being*.

Be still and know that I am God.
Be still and know that I am.
Be still and know.
Be still.
Be.

For a moment, we'd sit in that space of *being* until a student pressed Play on the CD player, and Danielle Rose's song "God Is" filled the room.[8] The first few notes always brought tears as I felt wholly seen, known, and loved in the stillness. Far beyond what I had been taught to understand about God, these poetic lyrics revealed the intimacy with which God shows up in our everyday lives, threaded through the ordinary. After years of struggling with the idea of God as a Father, this song (sung by a woman) introduced me to an ever-expansive, immanent, transcendent, mystical God who saw my searching and met me in the present moment. That's when I began to understand God was everywhere around and within me.

As I listen to this song now, I'm struck by how it beautifully echoes this seven-stage journey. These new seeds of God's presence within and around took root during that semester, which was both awkward and filled with additional layers of heartache. Friends were scattered, and I was three hours from the only city I knew. My mom moved across the country to be with her fiancé shortly after moving me onto campus. My sister planned to live with our biological father through high school and would call me some nights when she felt afraid of him. I struggled with depression and was grieving the hope of ever having a relationship with my biological father. This semester stripped me of the familiar and ushered me into one of the most painful seasons of my life.

And yet, this prayer of stillness, of knowing that God is God (and I am not), especially through such a tumultuous season, offered space for healing. As I participated in it, my soul was given room to break open and heal.

Years later, in 2018, with shaky hands and a hefty dose of imposter syndrome, I emailed Phileena Heuertz to ask her to be my spiritual director. She agreed, and in our first meeting, after a brief introduction, she invited me to close my eyes, take a few deep breaths, and tune into my heart, mind, and body. Then she said, "I now invite you to repeat after me . . ."

Be still and know that I am God.
Be still and know that I am.
Be still and know.
Be still.
Be.

Before she even finished the first line, my throat tightened and my heart broke open as my body remembered this prayer from years before. Phileena didn't know my history with it, and yet, we were reciting it together over the phone. After fifteen years of slowly pressing harder and harder on my accelerator, I'd been brought back to one of the most grounding practices for my soul: praying the "Be Still" prayer.[9] What a gift.

As you consider how to integrate this prayer, you may begin your centering prayer practice with it or set a reminder to recite it once a day. Perhaps you could integrate it as a communal prayer with family or a small group as I did in college. Regardless of how it's woven into your life, this practice is powerful in helping us move into and be with stillness.

Stillness in Sacred Reading—Lectio Divina

I first heard of Lectio Divina from a student in a Spirituality in Social Work Practice course I taught. Each student was assigned a day to begin the class with a short meditation practice of their choice, which included a yoga session, labyrinth walk, creating prayer boxes, and more. One student even offered a meditation that ended with her beautifully singing Gungor's song "The Great Homesickness."[10]

One week, one of my students led us through Lectio Divina, which is Latin for "divine reading."[11] Having chosen the story of Jesus's encounter with the Samaritan woman at the well (John 4:1–26), she invited us to listen through the story three times. First, she read the scripture, inviting us to hear the whole story and listen for any words or phrases that stood out. In the second reading, she invited us to pay attention to the word or phrase that initially jumped out, reflect on it, and respond by silently praying and sitting in stillness with God. Finally, in the third reading, she invited us to rest in the wholeness of the story with gratitude for the gift of God speaking through the sacred text. With each reading, we were invited to deepen our presence and ability to be still with the text.

Oftentimes, we read our sacred texts in a hurry, checking it off our to-do list like an errand but never allowing it to transform us. The practice of Lectio Divina allows stillness to enter the equation and creates space for the Sacred within to speak through the text. Concluding this practice, we're invited to *rest* in the story with a sense of gratitude, further supporting this inner stillness.

The Stillness of Sobriety

Like many others, addiction runs in my family, and more specifically, on *both* sides of my family of origin. Alcohol is the primary numbing agent in my family, but other addictive tendencies include overuse of sugar and caffeine as well as behavioral addictions to excessive work, materialism, money, power, and control.

I'm not at all immune to addiction, either, whether it's to substances or behaviors. Over the years, I've struggled with drinking too much wine, spending too much time on social media, devoting too much time to work, buying too much unnecessary stuff, eating too much food, and too often choosing busy over being. Why? Because in any moment of stillness, pain surfaced, and I'd do anything to numb or avoid it.

Some of this became clear as I was serving in the recovery ministry. As Seth Haines writes in his recovery book, *The Book of Waking Up*, "Waking gives way to waking, which gives way to waking, which gives way to waking," and I found this to be true.[12] The recovery ministry woke me up to my addiction to people-pleasing, performing, and perfecting, which woke me up to my addiction with social media and work, which woke me up to my dependency on alcohol to curb the stress. And these wakings are sure to give way to more.

In spring 2020, ironically two weeks before the world shut down for the COVID-19 pandemic, I wrote a Lenten reflection about quitting busyness.[13] I realized maintaining a perpetual state of *go* kept me unaware of so many other numbing tactics. Peeling back the busyness began to reveal other unhealthy mechanisms I used to cope with the stress of life.

It also helped me begin to see a truth Dr. Brené Brown taught me as an MSW student in her classroom and through her writing. She asserted that, "We cannot selectively numb emotions. When we numb the painful emotions, we also numb the positive emotions."[14] I began to realize that by dulling pain, heartache, and grief, I was experiencing a duller sense of joy, love, and peace. Failing to fully experience these positive emotions, I'd return to old habits to strive and hustle for the joy, love, and peace I had numbed.

As I've learned, the sober life is characterized by practicing intentional stillness, feeling the whole spectrum of emotions and pains of life as they surface, one moment at a time and to the best of our ability. As Richard Rohr notes:

> We shouldn't try to get rid of our own pain until we've learned what it has to teach. When we can hold our pain consciously and trustfully (and not project it elsewhere), we find ourselves in a very special liminal space. Here we are open to learning and breaking through to a much deeper level of faith and consciousness. Please trust me on this. We must all *carry the cross of our own reality* until God transforms us through it. *These are the wounded healers of the world, and healers who have fully faced their wounds are the only ones who heal anyone else.*[15]

But you cannot hold your pain consciously and trustfully when you're moving at a breakneck speed. Stillness is necessary to truly hold pain, and from my experience, actively participating in sobriety helps this process. It also makes room for gratitude and contentment.

Evening Stillness—Gratitude and Contentment

Just as I begin my day with centering prayer, I close it with gratitude. I began this intentional practice of gratitude in 2008 after reading Dr. Robert Emmons's book *Thanks: How Practicing Gratitude Can Make You Happier.*[16] Emmons argues that a regular practice of gratitude is powerful for our mental and physical health. And through his follow-up book, *Gratitude Works! A 21-Day Program for Creating Emotional Prosperity*, I discovered practices to regularly engage gratitude.[17] So I started experimenting with the practice in my own life, from integrating it on drives to work to keeping a gratitude journal to regularly practicing it at dinner with my family. And as helpful as all these practices were in one way or another, one practice of daily gratitude stuck.

As soon as my head hits the pillow each night, I turn to gratitude, naming everything I'm thankful for until I drift to sleep. And every night, my gratitude for the gifts in my life both humbles and overwhelms me. What's more, this practice stills my body, mind, heart, and spirit, moving me into a place of contentment and rest.

The intentional practice of gratitude forces us to still ourselves and remember the gifts that we have received. And the practice of gratitude reminds us that we often have more than we may realize and that we are enough. Through this practice, we begin operating from a place of enoughness instead of scarcity within ourselves. We come to realize that we don't need to hustle to prove our worth. Instead, we can be still and receive the goodness we've been given.

Stillness can be an act of resistance for the helper who is often pressured by others and by themselves to avoid being still. By incorporating stillness practices—whether those listed above or others that you find to be helpful—you give yourself the space to see God in and around you, and to listen to the still, small voice within. As Henri Nouwen says, "You have to be still and wait so that you can realize that God is not in the earthquake, the storm, or the lightning, but in the gentle breeze with which he touches your back."[18] And when you encounter God in and around you, when you experience God's healing, you're better able to see God's presence in others. This is why stillness is a critical practice of Namaste Theory. It continues to open up space to experience the Sacred in us and around us.

Stillness teaches us to surrender and experience God. It's that experience that allows us to see. What do I mean? Let's explore the next movement of this journey: See.

Reflection Exercises

What are some ways you're cultivating stillness in your life? What are some ways you're resisting it? Are there ways in which surrounding systems, communities, or ways of being either do or do not support stillness? Journal about your responses to each question.

Select one practice in this chapter to try this week. After you practice it, journal about your experience with this practice.

Reflect upon the practice of sobriety and think about what substances and/or behaviors you turn to when you're struggling with pain (e.g., shame, anger, fear, grief). Spend a moment identifying one way in which you numb pain and nonjudgmentally hold still space to become more aware of it.

CHAPTER 8

See

what is the greatest lesson a woman should learn

that since day one
she's already had everything she needs within herself
it's the world that convinced her she did not[1]

—rupi kaur

Like many Gen Xers and millennials, I grew up watching *Mister Rogers' Neighborhood*. I sang "Won't You Be My Neighbor?" with him at the beginning of every show.[2] I leaned in as he interacted with Mr. McFeely, several friends and puppets, and a tank full of fish. The show's concept was simple, and yet it offered some of the most profound lessons I've learned and created a soft spot in my heart for Fred Rogers. In fact, after nighttime prayers each evening, my kids and I sing his song "It's Such a Good Feeling" together to close the day.[3]

In February 2018, I stepped down from serving in the recovery ministry to focus on my own therapy. The space allowed me, Callie, and Oliver to have Wednesday nights together, as Cory continued to serve. We ended up turning Wednesdays into "Mister Rogers Night," eating pizza in the living room while watching old reruns of the show.

Watching this show as an adult helped me see the lessons were as much for grown-ups as children. Mister Rogers taught us to slow down and take the time to imagine, wonder, and learn. He taught us to be curious and humble and to celebrate our differences. He taught us to create, play, and sing. And more than anything, Mister Rogers taught us to love ourselves and others.

My fascination with the iconic television educator was only heightened by these weekly rerun dates with my kids. In 2019, I came across a clip from an episode in which he sang his famous tune, "It's You I Like."[4] At the heart of the song is a message from Mister Rogers that he likes us for who we are, exactly as we are in this very moment, aside from our appearances, clothing, or material possessions. After singing the song in this particular clip, he said, "And that's true. And you'll find that the people who love you best are the ones you learn the most from. And the more they teach you and the more you learn, the better feeling you have about yourself and the world we live in."

Mister Rogers made a singular truth abundantly clear: he liked us. No strings attached. And there can be no doubt where he got this idea. I'm positive this Presbyterian minister believed that was exactly the way God likes us, simply for who we are. I wholeheartedly agree. In fact, I believe God *loves* us for who we are. I believe God *made* us by love, out of God's love, to love others and ourselves in this exact same way.

I hope by the end of this chapter, you will see it for yourself.

Seeing the Divine Spark

When we become still, we're positioned to fully see the Sacred within. It's a bold statement, I know, and you may be thinking, "But I *have* sensed the Sacred within, even in the midst of running hard and fast for so long!" I believe you. The truth is, even when I've been moving too fast, I've caught glimpses of the Sacred. Still, it's like driving past a beautiful flower. At 25 miles per hour you might notice it, but you cannot fully appreciate it. In fact, to fully appreciate it you have to come to a stop, get out of the car, and spend some time with the flower.

When we slow down, steady ourselves in the slower rhythm, and become still, we can see God in and around us. And it's a journey that's ongoing, one we have to engage on a regular basis.

So, what is the goal of this *seeing* stage? Is it about seeing the Sacred in the world around you? Yes. Is it about seeing the Sacred in others? Yes. But most importantly, this stage offers the space to see the divine spark, the Sacred, within yourself. By seeing this divine spark within ourselves, we can better see the Sacred in others and the world.

The notion of the Sacred or the divine spark within you exists across many religious traditions. It's prominently displayed in the Roman Catholic tradition of my youth through the image of the Sacred Heart of Jesus.[5] In that image, Jesus points to his radiant, burning, Sacred Heart, a symbol of his deep love for God and all of humanity. In some moments of stillness, I've experienced this kind of mysterious, radiant light source, this divine spark, within the center of my own chest, humming with energy, love, and eternity that grounds me. It's God with me, in me. It's the breath of life and an infinite source of what so many of us are seeking: *pure, unconditional love.* And if it's in me, it's in you too.

In Ecclesiastes 3:11 (NIV), Solomon wrote that God has "set eternity in the human heart." This eternity within our hearts—the divine spark—invites us to wake up and see the Sacred within. Seeing this spark, holding space for it, and surrendering to it without an agenda or any strings attached results in transformation. We cannot help but change once we truly see the image of God inside us. And once we see God in ourselves, we'll begin to see God within the whole spectrum of humanity. And in that way, we begin to see the whole spectrum of humanity within ourselves.

Within Taoism, which doesn't worship God in the way Abra-hamic traditions do and dates back to around 500 B.C., there's an understanding of an energy source called the Tao, or the way of the universe.[6] As the Tao Te Ching teaches,

> There was something formless and perfect
> before the universe was born.
> It is serene. Empty.
> Solitary. Unchanging.
> Infinite. Eternally present.
> It is the mother of the universe.
> For lack of a better name,
> I call it the Tao.
>
> It flows through all things,
> inside and outside, and returns
> to the origin of all things.[7]

This process of seeking the Sacred within will move us toward a nondualistic way of being, away from categorizing everything as good or bad, right or wrong, and toward the mystery of paradox. In fact, moving further into this stage of *See*, we will need to face the complexity and paradox within us.

A Pause to Honor Grief and Recognize Our Motivations

As we begin to see the Sacred, we'll also become aware of the Sacred we've missed within ourselves and others. How many days did we fly through an overpacked schedule, thinking about what's ahead or what happened yesterday, without once *being* in the moment? How many moments were spent focusing on distractions rather than the image of God in us and in others? How many times did we choose accomplishments and achievements over presence and play? How many unpromised days, moments, or encounters with the Sacred did we miss?

Take a deep breath with me here. We have to hold space for all of this.

We cannot go back or hit a "redo" button. What's done is done. So we're invited to nonjudgmentally observe what we're becoming aware of and *feel the grief* that's surfacing, rather than numb, avoid, bypass, repress, or justify it.

Sit with the pain with open palms, breathe deep, notice the emotions, and allow the grief to be a teacher. Remind yourself you were doing the best you could with what you had. Extend grace toward yourself and forgive yourself, trusting in a Divine Love that extends grace and forgiveness toward you. (If you need help sitting with what's surfacing, please reach out to a mental health care provider or spiritual director to journey beside you.)

After we grieve what we missed while operating at our previous pace, we also need to grieve the illusion that everything we've done to help, serve, or care for others has been good, healing, or helpful. This may be hard to receive, but as the well-known aphorism goes, "The road to hell is paved with good intentions."[8] Having good intentions in serving others doesn't mean we're actually engaging in serving others, nor are our efforts always good, healing, or helpful, and they may have even hurt others. It's important to pause and see the spectrum of potential and actual outcomes.

To be clear, helping others get access to lifesaving necessities is good. Saving lives and healing others is good. Meeting others' tangible human needs is good. Fighting against systemic injustice and oppression is good. Advocating for others' well-being is good. And yet, if we are not paying curiously close attention to our inner landscapes—including our motivations, biases, beliefs, and blind spots—we may be helping others to serve our own agendas, running the risk of causing pain in the process. Again, as Fr. Richard Rohr says, "If we do not transform the pain, we will most assuredly transmit it."[9]

In his book *From the Inside Out*, spiritual director Ryan Kuja demonstrates how helping can sometimes hurt within the context of Christian missionary work.[10] While listing several historical horrors from colonialism, he notes a current of harm done in the name of helping others, especially when the "helpers" operate with a lack of cultural humility and self-awareness:

> Everywhere I went [including Haiti, South Africa, India, Nicaragua, and El Salvador], I encountered more faith-based sojourners from North America doing various types of mission work with the best of intentions, all the while remaining unaware of their true impact on local people and their own need to know themselves, their own need for saving and transformation. Over and over I saw people committed to all sorts of good work—community development, anti–human trafficking, clean water, education for youth, discipleship, church planting—who were unintentionally, and often unconsciously, acting out the white savior narrative, grasping for power over others, using the poor as objects of their compassion, and believing they could transform people without having been transformed themselves.[11]

We must pay attention to why we're doing what we do as helpers. Some of our reasons for helping are obvious, but we all have blind spots. Although our spiritual and mental health journeys influence our motivations, there are three additional considerations.

Programs for Happiness, Lies of Identity, and Our Personality

The first consideration in determining why we do what we do comes from the work of Fr. Thomas Keating. He writes about "three essential biological needs" in early childhood that, if the child is deprived of these, can become insatiable "programs for happiness," which are as follows: security and survival, power and control, and affection and esteem.[12] These programs are tied to the childhood wounds from which we developed attachments and aversions related to people, things, or situations. They helped us to cope, comfort, or protect ourselves from the pain we suffered early in life.

Nodding to Kuja's experience, we may be unintentionally and unconsciously seeking those programs for happiness in how we serve others. For me, this can show up in my overfunctioning around work, social media, perfection, and people-pleasing. My inner work requires paying attention to how my attachments to affection, control, and security can sneak into what I do, helping me carefully discern what is mine to do. How do I do this? I *practice* remembering that I'm enough and loved as I am, aside from the things I do (including for others). I remind myself that control is an illusion, death is immanent, and each day is an unpromised gift. And as a tangible reminder to keep my tasks in perspective and lean into humility, the following words are written across my planner: "I am not in control. I cannot fix everything. Do what is mine to do and trust it is enough."

Second, Henri Nouwen indicates we're often motivated by three lies of identity: *I am what I have*, *I am what I do*, and *I am what others say or think about me*.[13] Hustling to prove our worth based on what we have or do, or on others' opinions of us, is tempting, but the reality is we are not defined by them. We are unconditionally loved. To counter these lies, I hung a sign above my desk that reads, "I am not what I have. I am not what I do. I am not what others think of me. I am Beloved."

The third consideration is that transformation occurs when we come to know ourselves in all our complexity, including our personality. The Big Five personality traits, Myers-Briggs Type Indicator, or Enneagram can help us with this.[14] When we begin to better understand deeper facets of our personality, including our communication style, our approaches to navigating conflict, willingness to try new things, well-formed habits, and even the ways we act in social settings, we gain a more nuanced view of our motivations.

Through contemplative practices, we can nonjudgmentally see and repeatedly release our attachments to these programs for happiness, lies of identity, and personality struggles so we don't remain stuck in negative cycles, particularly when we're attempting to help others. Recognizing and releasing these things are necessary to begin seeing our inherent belovedness and to quit hustling for our worth. As Phileena Heuertz wrote,

> As we grow in self-awareness we often realize that some of our reactions to present circumstances are actually reactions to past events that are buried in our unconscious. . . . Even some of our best deeds can be laced with violence that we are asleep to. Contemplation purifies our actions. Through contemplation we are able to confront the darkness of our personalities and the emotional investments we have made in false "programs for happiness." As a result we open ourselves to the possibilities of experiencing interior freedom instead of pursuing power and control, divine love instead of craving the affection and esteem of others, [and the] presence of God instead of clinging to security and survival.[15]

Namaste Theory and these corresponding stages guide help- ers to see the Sacred within, but they also help us see our shadows. Through facing and understanding these shadows, we can move away from unconsciously chasing our programs for happiness, internalizing the lies of identity that shape us, as well as avoiding the darker sides of our personality, and instead, we can move toward transformation.

Transformation

As we clearly see the complexity within ourselves, a natural trans- formation begins to unfold. Again, we cannot force, control, or pre- dict this unfolding but are invited to surrender to the process as it begins.

I experienced a moment of this kind of transformation at a retreat in 2018. On a beautiful September day, I decided to skip a yoga session to walk the labyrinth.[16] As I approached the tree beside it, I heard the familiar voice of imposter syndrome.

What am I doing here? I've walked a labyrinth before, but I feel . . . awkward. Maybe I should have gone to the yoga class.

Yet, a magnetic pull held me there with an inner nudge that said, "Yes. Be here. Get ready." I sat at the bench, took a moment to pray and be still, and looked down to find a single monarch but- terfly wing, which reminded me of my favorite passage in Huertz's *Pilgrimage of a Soul*:

> The caterpillar can't make herself become the butterfly—that kind of change requires confinement, solitude, stillness, and receptivity to something bigger than herself. This is how trans- formation is made possible. Remember, we cannot make ourselves grow; but we can choose to submit to or resist the process. And though much growth takes place in our active

lives, all elements of creation are subject to contemplative stillness as an integral part of growth and transformation. The
butterfly does not become the magnificent, colorful crea-
ture by a fury of activity. She submits to the confinement of
the chrysalis—womb-like, tomb-like. She is still. She rests.
She receives. She submits to a work more glorious than she
could have ever conjured up for herself.[17]

This butterfly wing felt like a divine nod. I was where I needed to
be. I stepped to the edge of the labyrinth, took a deep breath, and
began to walk the path.

With each step that I took, random memories surfaced from
my childhood. I paused when I needed to be with a memory, then
released it and continued. I considered the turning-point decisions
and experiences throughout my life—moments that drew me closer
to or further from the Divine—while continuing on the path
toward the center. It felt as if shipwrecks were surfacing in my soul,
but I gave each the space and margin to be felt and honored.

After making the final turn to face the center of the labyrinth,
I paused, took a deep breath, and slowly moved forward. Crossing
the center's threshold, I closed my eyes and felt the sun's warmth
on my face. I breathed deep and knelt down, somehow sensing I
was suddenly on holy ground. A brilliant, golden light grew bright,
even with my eyes closed, and I wept.

As clear as could be, I heard deep within my soul: *"Wake up. . . .
I made you, child. I created you and I love you. You don't need to do
anything for that love—it's here. I could not love you any more.
I could not love you any less. I love you as you are."*

A steady stream of tears fell as I felt this Divine Love reorder
me and root me into a grounded state of being. I knew then that I
was loved *as I am*. Not as I could be or once was or should be. Noth-

ing I could do would alter this Love and it would never change or leave me.

I sat in this space as long as I could until it was time to leave; unfortunately, I couldn't stay in the center forever. With my face covered in tears, feeling both grounded and free, I began the slow, winding walk out of the labyrinth. I mindfully held my hands out in front of the center of my body the entire time as if I were carrying a gift—the gift of knowing that no matter what bends appeared in my path, I was loved and created because God *loved* me and *wanted* to create me. In that moment, my core belief system deeply shifted into a simple statement: *I believe I am loved.*

Isn't this the message we all need to hear? It was a transformative message, but like the butterfly's transformation, I couldn't have forced the experience to happen through a fury of activity. Only by submitting to the solitude of the retreat, the stillness within, the receptivity to something bigger than me, the trust to follow the nudge to skip yoga and go to the labyrinth, and the grounded willingness to surrender to a process beyond my control was I able to receive this gift of fully knowing my identity as God's Beloved. Only then could I fully see the Sacred within, just as I am.

Practices That Help Us to More Clearly See

Especially for helpers, it may seem easier to practice seeing the Sacred in others than in ourselves. Why? First, when we devote all our attention toward others, we don't have time or energy to look inward. Second, the addiction to affirmation, accolades, and affection can keep us looking outside of ourselves for approval instead of excavating what's within. There's no public recognition for doing the inner work—it is slow, unseen, and patient work, rewarded with a quiet, intimate connection with the Sacred. Third, many of us have been raised in faith communities that constantly tell us to look up and outside of ourselves (at times, even discouraging looking inward) rather than teaching us to be with and tend to our inner landscape. Pairing all of that with a fast-paced culture, the practice of patiently looking inward can seem impossible.

Until we've become fully aware of the Sacred within ourselves, I'm afraid that what we see in others is a distorted image of the Divine, reflecting only as much clarity as we've seen within ourselves, particularly if we're still hustling. But here's the good news: there are practices to help. And as we engage these practices to see the Sacred within ourselves, we'll be positioned to recognize the Sacred in others.

Contemplation

The overall practice of contemplation is ongoing. More specifically,

> Contemplation is a panoramic, receptive awareness whereby you take in all that the situation, the moment, the event offers, without judging, eliminating, or labeling anything up or down, good or bad. It is *a pure and positive gaze*, unattached to outcome or critique. . . . [It] is about receiving and being present to the moment, to the *now*, without judgment, analysis, or critique, without your ego deciding whether you like it or not. *Reality does not need you to like it in order to be reality.* This is a much more holistic knowing, where your mind, heart, soul, and senses are open and receptive to the moment *just as it is*, which allows you . . . to hold everything—both the attractive and the unpleasant—together in one accepting gaze.[18]

Each of the movements described in the previous chapters is meant to draw us to contemplate the Sacred within.

In Speed, we recognized the fast pace of our lives, our honest risk of burnout, and our need to move from precontemplation to contemplation as it relates to hustling for our worth.

In Slow, we learned to adjust our speed in order to have the space to contemplate the Sacred.

In Steady, we learned how tuning in, receiving support, resting, and practicing curiosity and surrender allow us to interact with the Sacred.

In Still, we learned how centering prayer, nonjudgmental self-observation, the "Be Still" prayer, and Lectio Divina provide a lived experience with the Sacred.

At this point in the journey of seeking the Sacred, we see what's always existed within us—the divine spark—and submit to a healing beyond our control. As Thomas Keating explains:

> To submit to the divine therapy [in contemplation and, more specifically, centering prayer] is something we owe to ourselves and the rest of humanity. If we don't allow the Spirit of God to address the deep levels of our attachments to ourselves and to our programs for happiness, we will pour into the world the negative elements of our self-centeredness, adding to the conflicts and social disasters that come from overidentifying with the biases and prejudices of our particular culture and upbringing. This is becoming more important as we move into a global culture . . . .[19]

We cannot help or fix our way into healing as part of this "divine therapy" Keating describes with a flurry of activity. Yes, there are studies that indicate helping others produces positive emotions and outcomes; however, *healing* our compulsive fixation on security, control, or affection requires a deeper journey.[20] Like the butterfly's transformation, our inner healing from these attachments occurs beyond our efforts. The practice of contemplation is what positions us for and supports us through this healing.

So, how do we practice contemplation so that we can see the Sacred within? First, we must understand that we cannot hustle our way into healing or hurry to experience the Sacred. Contemplation simply (and not so simply) requires a consistent showing up to the contemplative practices of our choice without an agenda, goal, or timeline. This patient consistency creates space to *practice* receptive awareness, surrender, and being present to the moment.

By doing this, we begin to seek the Sacred within the present moment. We pay attention to how the Sacred shows up in the most unexpected of ways and lean into the surprises with curiosity and childlike faith. After bearing witness to the gift of each surprise, we release it with open palms. Over time, this will ripple out from our contemplative practices into our active lives as we serve others and seek the Sacred in the world around us.

It is truly as easy and as difficult as that, fellow traveler.

If you need help moving into this space of contemplation, Mary Mrozowski's "Welcoming Prayer" can be a useful guide.[21] As Mrozowski says, "To welcome and to let go is one of the most radically loving, faith-filled gestures we can make in each moment of each day. It is an open-hearted embrace of all that is in ourselves and in the world."[22] As a social worker and trauma survivor, I know there is darkness and evil in the world, and of course, I'm not suggesting we embrace that darkness. As Richard Rohr clarifies, this is not about "suggesting that we welcome or accept abuse, trauma, or oppression, but rather our feelings around those incidents. We then become empowered to take necessary action more freely, creatively, and lovingly."[23]

As a reminder to embrace all that is in the world and in myself, including my feelings about the darker aspects of the world, I've hung the following prayer above my desk, just next to Callie's drawing described in chapter 6:

> *Gently become aware of your body*
> *and your interior state.*
>
> *Welcome, welcome, welcome.*
> *I welcome everything that comes to me in this moment*
> *because I know it is for my healing.*
> *I welcome thoughts, feelings, emotions,*
> *persons, situations, and conditions.*
>
> *I let go of my desire for security.*
> *I let go of my desire for approval.*
> *I let go of my desire for control.*
>
> *I let go of my desire to change any*
> *situation, condition,*
> *person, or myself.*
>
> *I open to the love and presence of God and*
> *the healing action and grace within.*[24]

The heart of this prayer is truly about letting go and *being* with what is in the present moment to the best of our ability.

Sacred Writing

In the last chapter, I noted how solitude and silence dance alongside stillness. To connect with the Sacred or Divine within ourselves, it helps to create spaces to step away from the flurry of our active, social, and noisy lives. We must learn to exist within ourselves, separate from those around us or the distractions pulling for our attention.

While many of the previously mentioned practices help me connect with the Sacred in solitude and silence, my regular writing practice is the most helpful. Unable to write faster than I can think, I'm forced to slowly look inward as I spend time alone with my thoughts and a pen or keyboard. Without prompts, I allow any emotion, thought, or sensation to surface. As author Allison Fallon notes in *The Power of Writing It Down*, "Writing is not *just* writing. Writing is prayer, spirituality, self-discovery, communication, therapy, connection."[25] Gentle music sometimes helps me move through surfacing emotions, but the removal of distractions is the heart of silence.

What do I discover in these spaces? Anything and everything. Work anxieties. Long-forgotten memories. Things that spark gratitude. New ways of understanding complex topics. A deeper appreciation for each sunrise. And as I write, I reconnect with the quiet hum of the Divine. In this regular space of writing in solitude and silence, which often follows my centering prayer practice, I move out of the way and let whatever needs to surface show up in my writing. And this practice of writing has changed me. As the great Persian poet and Sufi mystic Rumi wrote:

> In your light I learn how to love.
> In your beauty, how to make poems.
>
> You dance inside my chest,
> where no one sees you,
>
> but sometimes I do,
> and that sight becomes this art.[26]

Writing—like other forms of creativity, art, and music—creates space to see the Sacred. Try it as one of your seeing practices.

Whether you set aside an hour once a week or ten minutes a day, please set your phone aside, find a quiet space to be alone, and spend some time writing without a goal or agenda.

You may be surprised by what surfaces.

You may even find the Sacred dancing inside your chest.

Namaste: A Call to See

Before closing this chapter, let's ground ourselves back in Namaste Theory. Remember, this theory, which is rooted in research related to helping professionals, recognizes the importance of seeking the Sacred within ourselves in order to see the Sacred in others. It helps bring clarity as we go out to help, serve, and care for others.

I noted earlier that I read Gabrielle Earnshaw's compilation of Henri Nouwen's writings in *You Are the Beloved* each morning before practicing centering prayer. Quite poetically, the following words by Henri Nouwen are assigned on my last day around the sun each year. The passage is stunningly entitled "Stay Awake," and it so beautifully embodies Namaste Theory.

> The practice of contemplative prayer is the discipline by which we begin to "see" the living God dwelling in our own hearts. Careful attentiveness to the One who makes a home in the privileged center of our being gradually leads to recognition. As we come to know and love the Father of our hearts we give ourselves over to this incredible Presence who takes possession of all our senses. By the discipline of prayer we are awakened and opened to God within, who enters into our heartbeat and our breathing, into our thoughts and emotions, our hearing, seeing, touching, and tasting. It is by being awake to this God within that we also find the Presence in the world around us. Here we are again in front of the secret. It is not that we see God in the world, but that God-with-us recognizes God in the

world. God speaks to God, Spirit speaks to Spirit, heart speaks
to heart.

Contemplation, therefore, is a participating in the divine self-
recognition. The divine Spirit alive in us makes our world
transparent for us and opens our eyes to the presence of the
divine Spirit in all that surrounds us. It is with our heart of
hearts that we see the heart of the world. . . . [27]

As we awaken to and see God within us, we recognize God
around us, especially in the people around us. We begin to live into
what Nambiar teaches us about Namaste.

The Divine within me honors the Divine within you.

The Sacred within me bows to the Sacred within you.

The God within me recognizes the God within you.

Fellow helper, for a moment, imagine we're together in your living room. Imagine me looking into your eyes, asking you to see
the infinite worth within yourself as a reflection of the infinite
worth within me. With your whole heart and soul, hear me as I say:

Wake up, friend. Wake up. Wake up. Wake up and see.

See the divine spark within!

See God in and around you!

*See all the layers God threaded together within you into a
whole, beautiful, stunning, miraculous you!*

*You are alive and breathing and fully human and behold the
Divine within you!*

Dear friend, believe me when I tell you that you are the Beloved.

Breathe this truth deep into your being. Receive it. Embody it.
When you do, you can finally give unconditional love to others

because you've finally awakened to that infinite, unconditional love in yourself. This, my friend, is how we begin to wholly love our neighbors as ourselves, just as Jesus asked us to do in each of the four Gospels.

So, friend, stay awake and see the Sacred love within yourself. You are so worth it.

Reflection Exercises

As you move through this stage of the journey, take a moment to honor the grief that rises when you think about the ways you've served out of your attachment to the various programs for happiness, lies of identity, or your ego. What are some ways you're beginning to see how you may have unintentionally hurt others in your efforts to help, even when you weren't aware of it at the time?

Is there one sacred moment that stands out in your life, some time when you've experienced a deep knowing of your identity as Beloved or where you felt deeply connected to God or your Higher Power?

Similar to the last chapter, select one practice in this chapter to try this week. After practicing it, journal about your experience.

CHAPTER 9

Shift

*[Love is] the will to extend one's self for the purpose
of nurturing one's own or another's spiritual growth.*[1]

—Dr. M. Scott Peck

Once we see and become aware of the image of God within ourselves and the love that we did nothing to earn, we cannot unsee this truth. Still, our human condition prevents us from staying in that space of awe, surrender, and deep knowing. Childhood wounds still surface. Schedules continue to fill up, and our to-do lists will occasionally get out of control. Loved ones still misunderstand us from time to time. We still have bills to pay, responsibilities to tend to, and stressors to navigate. And of course, well-formed habits resurface to cope with these difficulties, causing us to sometimes lose sight of the Sacred within. This is why it is so important to practice remaining mindful of the stages of seeking the Sacred.

Change takes time, and without intention or attention, it's easy to lose sight and return to our old ways. Working the Twelve Steps and showing up to my centering prayer chair each morning have helped me realize that connection to my inherent belovedness happens through "living one day at a time; enjoying one moment at a time," as the Serenity Prayer says.[2]

Living into this truth daily is so important to me, I had my own reminders tattooed on my wrists. If we ever meet, you'll notice the words "be still" on my left wrist and "beloved" on my right wrist.

And when my palms are together and facing up, I am reminded to, "be still, beloved," with the tiny heart that Callie drew (described in chapter 6) on the inside of both wrists. These words and tiny hearts remind me to keep my palms up and to not miss sacred moments on account of my own temptations to speed up, do more, people-please, and achieve.

Although this is how I remind myself of God's presence, of my inherent worth, and of my need to surrender, I'd encourage you to identify a way to offer yourself these reminders too. You are worth receiving them.

Fellow helper, when we see we are the Beloved *as we are*, we show up to the gift of our life, release control, allow our life to unfold before us, do what is ours to do, and humbly surrender to what the next moment holds. And in deeply knowing, feeling, and embodying our belovedness, we begin to see the inherent belovedness within others.

When we see the Sacred within everything and everyone, our awareness of the Sacred exponentially grows. And the more we practice seeking the Sacred, the more vibrant God's presence and work in the world appear. As Pope Francis notes, "The universe unfolds in God, who fills it completely. Hence, there is a mystical meaning to be found in a leaf, in a mountain trail, in a dewdrop, in a poor person's face. The ideal is not only to pass from the exterior to the interior to discover the action of God in the soul, but also to discover God in all things. Saint Bonaventure teaches us that 'contemplation deepens the more we feel the working of God's grace within our hearts, and the better we learn to encounter God in creatures outside ourselves.'"[3]

Although we see the Sacred more clearly around us upon seeing it within ourselves, we may find that it's sometimes easier to see the Sacred in others. Other times, it seems easier to see the Sacred within ourselves. Both forms of seeking the Sacred are necessary and can teach us about the other if we let them.

Recognizing the teachings that call us to love our enemies, I often find it much easier to see the Sacred within myself than in those who have hurt me, shamed me, violated my boundaries, silenced me, or taken advantage of me. (Which is not to say we bypass the pain by offering easy platitudes or looking for silver linings in the hurt; for more on this, see Dr. Jesse Fox's work on spiritual bypassing.[4]) On a similar note, when I'm my own enemy, personally wrapped up in anger, fear, and shame toward myself, it's nearly impossible to find the Sacred within myself.

But when I give myself to the inner work of seeing the Sacred within myself and others, I inch toward all my neighbors as part of the "universal community."[5] It's easier to see that we are all doing the best we can with what we have (resources, information, beliefs, access, support, experiences, and so on) and, from that sense of grace, there's a deep love for my neighbor, myself, and even my enemy. It's not always easy, but in this way of seeing, there's a sort of shift. Two shifts, actually.

The Two Shifts

When we pursue Namaste, the first shift involves our entire being shifting in response to the Sacred within ourselves. Our decisions, behaviors, thoughts, emotions, and ways of being transform. How could they not in response to awakening to this profound truth and discovering the Sacred within ourselves?

The second shift is simply an outworking of the first and involves our views toward and interactions with others. When we see the inherent divine spark within ourselves, the spark we did nothing to deserve or earn, we come to understand that every human has this divine spark in them, too. And when I say every human, I mean every human.

The Pope.

The politician you can't stand.

The quiet neighbor. The loud neighbor.

The multibillionaire CEO. The unemployed.

The hormone-raging teenager you're raising.

The advocate fighting against systemic injustice.

The peaceful newborn baby.

The elderly woman with Alzheimer's disease.

The prison inmate, the energetic PTA mom, the partner fighting symptoms of depression.

The transgender college student coming out to their family.

The agnostic who visits the lake, the woman who attends the synagogue, the man who attends the mosque.

The clients or patients or colleagues or students or customers or congregants or family members or loved ones you interact with every day.

Every single human bears the divine spark, the image of God within, even if they don't recognize it or if they call it another name. As we move deeper into Namaste Theory, we must practice seeing this divine spark within everyone around us.

Shifting in Response to Noticing the Sacred Within Ourselves

Have you ever watched a curling competition? In curling, the first player slides a large stone while two team members rush in front of it with curling brooms, sweeping the ice to reduce the friction and help the stone travel to the painted target called the house.[6] (Yes, this might be a gross oversimplification, but as someone who's never participated in this sport, this represents the depth of my understanding.)

My sense of watching curling is that, like many sports, it requires skill and calculation as well as surrender and trust in your teammates. Those with the brooms have no control over the first team member's throw of the stone. And once the stone is thrown, the first team member is still, having done their part to the best of their ability, trusting the sweepers to support the stone's path to the house.

This reminds me a lot of the journey of seeking the Sacred. There are intentional steps of discernment we take to slow down, set up structures that steady us, and practice stillness to see the Sacred within. But once we begin this inner work, something changes within us. We trust others to support our journey. For me, those include my family and friends who love me well, my health and mental health care providers, my pastor and spiritual director, and fellow travelers who teach me in the most unexpected of ways. Relying on them requires both surrender and trust.

This surrender and trust allow for a deep inner shift toward healing. Knowing that nurturing this sacredness takes time, we begin the process of unwinding a lifetime of negative thoughts, emotional patterns, and reckless behaviors we've mindlessly allowed to direct the script of our lives. We begin to own the parts of our healing that are ours to tend to and release what's beyond our control. We don't live under the need to hustle for our worth or the constant expectations of others but from our inherent identity as Beloved.

During this shift, true healing begins. Moving into this stage, I noticed that previous reactions to feelings of shame, anger, or fear were softening. Slowly, I'd catch an occasional and unexpected move toward curiosity rather than shame, tenderness rather than criticism, acceptance rather than control, and faith rather than certainty. For example, if I was running late to a meeting, I stopped automatically apologizing for being late to people-please and thanked them for their patience, recognizing there was a reason I was late. Or rather than continuing to wear clothing that left my body hurting by the end of the day (and berate my body for not fitting into them "perfectly"), I wore clothes that felt kind to my body.[7] Or if I missed a deadline, rather than imploding on myself and reiterating the shaming narrative of not being or doing enough, I let it go. And the shift toward these softer responses was becoming evident in the way I felt about myself.

In this shift, we also tune into our body, mind, and heart more naturally, discerning what our sensations, thoughts, and emotions are trying to teach us. We turn toward honoring them rather than stuffing and ignoring them (only for them to later come out sideways on a loved one). Practicing curiosity, we begin to prioritize creating margins to tend those sensations, thoughts, and emotions and practice lovingkindness toward ourselves, mindful of our inherent worth. We begin to discover in this shift that our speed is inherently regulated in ways that previously seemed impossible.

Recognizing the Sacred within ourselves ultimately unveils a new desire to receive and tend to the gift of our precious and sacred life. Healing from the years of hustling and hurry becomes a new priority for us as helpers, inviting us to experience life in ways our soul had been longing to encounter.

Not only does this healing impact us, it impacts the work we do with others as helpers. That's why this healing shift is the foundation of Namaste Theory. It allows us to experience the presence of the Sacred, recognizing its infusion into all areas of our life, and prepares us for the second shift.

Shifting in Response to Recognizing the Sacred in Others

Grounded in the experiential knowing that we are the Beloved and bear the image of God within, our hearts are prepared for the second shift. This shift allows us to see the inherent belovedness within others, regardless of their age, race, gender, sexual orientation, ability, religious affiliation, nationality, physical appearance, or any other layer of intersectionality. In fact, believing each person bears the image of God, we're invited to consider how various layers of intersectionality are representative of a much bigger, more inclusive, and widely diverse God than we may have previously been taught or ever could have imagined.

Over the last several years and through this nonlinear journey, I've experienced this shift firsthand. While I don't love traveling for work, I love the people-watching opportunities it allows. Fellow travelers visit the airport for a myriad of reasons—a vacation, a job interview, a work meeting, a cross-country move, a family reunion. People from across the globe walk the concourses, each representing a beautiful tapestry of experiences and expressions.

The day after the November 2016 election, the John Templeton Foundation flew me and some colleagues to Atlanta for a two-day meeting on the intersection of spirituality and mental health. It was a milestone opportunity for my career, and I was humbled by the gift to gather with this group, learn from them, share what I knew, and begin finding ways to collaborate across disciplines.

Because it was the day following this election, the whole travel experience felt surreal. There was a palpable sense of discomfort and shock in each airport: Waco, Dallas, and Atlanta. We all felt it, and it seemed everyone's eyes were darting around, wondering who was celebrating or grieving or afraid of or numb to the results.

Despite traveling a handful of times each year for work, I'd never shuffled alongside fellow travelers on a day that felt so suspended in time.

As I stepped off the plane from Waco and into the Dallas airport, I felt a nudge to start a new practice when I travel. As I walked the concourses, rode the monorails, and sat in restaurants or terminal seats, I began practicing seeking the image of God in that diverse group of fellow travelers. As I did, I repeated a simple mantra in my mind with each person I saw: *You bear the image of God.*

When they looked happy or joyful, it felt easy to sense their divine spark shining within them. When they appeared grumpy or rushed, it felt more difficult to sense their divine spark. Regardless of how they presented in that moment, I continued the practice to honor the surrounding diversity and to stretch my limited, human perspective of God in so many ways. Of course, they had no idea I was quietly doing this, which somehow made the process even more rewarding. It was like I was participating with God in some secret, divine scavenger hunt.

Now when I visit an airport, I consider them all: the Puerto Rican toddler; the older man in a wheelchair and the airport employee escorting him; the young Black woman; the anxious adolescent; the Muslim couple and their sleeping baby; the gay couple; the soccer team; the travelers wearing bold political attire; the businessman and businesswoman; the grieving man; the overstimulated child; the Asian American sergeant; the woman two chairs down from me playing Christian music really loud without headphones and taking selfies (true story); the faith leader; the airline captain; the flight attendant; the airport baristas and waiters; the college student studying; my flight neighbor fighting for armrest real estate to play a game on his phone while I type like a T-Rex for three hours (also a true story). Each is a beautiful, stunning, miraculous image-bearer of the Divine, whether they know it or not. They are on their own personal journey, and for one sacred moment in history, their journey has crossed paths with mine. And I've been given an invitation to notice.

Engaging this practice on that strange travel day in 2016 drastically changed how I see the image of God within others. That practice continues to impact my day-to-day life. Although airports offer layers of diversity that stretch me, humble me, and leave me curious about my fellow travelers, I apply the same practice in my everyday world, especially as a helper. Whether I'm teaching, facilitating a meeting, leading a research study, speaking to a group, or helping in the community, I'll occasionally catch myself asking questions about the people I'm helping, and even the people who are helping me.

Who are these images of God?

Whom and what do they love?

What secrets are they carrying?

What pain and hope coexist within them?

What was their childhood like and how did it shape who they are today?

What do they believe about life, humanity, and God?

What do they believe about themselves?

Have they woken up to the Sacred within themselves and within others?

Are they seeking the Sacred in this moment?

As I go into the world as a helper, I run across all kinds of different people with different perspectives, experiences, and layers of intersectionality. Sometimes I instantly connect with them or feel a sense of comfort. Sometimes I disagree with them or simply don't care for their personalities. Still, to the best of my ability, I try to remain mindful that the image of God is in them too. By doing so,

I'm reminded that they, too, have an inherent divine spark, which is a gift.

Practices That Help Us Shift

When you experience the shifts that come from seeing the Sacred in yourself and others, true empathy emerges. You are able to be gentler with yourself. You're able to better love your friends and family members. You can even begin to love your neighbor as yourself. But how do you support these shifts? I've discovered a few practices that might help.

Seeking the Sacred

The first is the practice of seeking the Sacred or the image of God within our neighbors and ourselves. Like the airport practice I described above, this can be done anywhere—at the grocery store, office, restaurant, coffee shop, place of worship, home, or driving around town. Take the time to notice those around you. With a contemplative prayer posture, quietly whisper these words in your heart as you see each person: *You bear the image of God.* (Note: You don't have to creep the other person out and stare at them as they walk by; a quick notice will do.)

At the same time, seek the image of God within yourself too. When you look in the mirror, remember that you embody one of nearly eight billion individuals who bear the image of God on the planet today. You hold the Sacred inside you, regardless of your faith tradition, experiences, nationalities, abilities, age, race, ethnicity, gender, sexual orientation, relationship and/or parental status, vocation, family of origin, access to resources, socioeconomic status, education, physical appearance, or skill sets. You are a part of God's beautifully diverse and complex presence in the world. Remind yourself of this truth every day.

Practicing Humility

Although humility is a characteristic or virtue, it can also be a practice. As described by psychologist Dr. Mark McMinn, "humility involves a reasonably accurate view of oneself, a concern for others, and an openness to various ideas."[8] The practice of this "reasonably accurate view of oneself" is critical for helpers.

This is *not* the same as self-abnegation, or the tendency to put ourselves down, make ourselves small, or view ourselves as less valuable, important, or worthy. Humility involves a balance of honoring our value alongside the value of others, recognizing that our ego isn't the center of the universe. In fact, in *The Science of Virtue*, Dr. McMinn outlines Dr. June Tangey's six dimensions of humility as follows:

1. Accurate view of oneself (neither too high nor too low)
2. Ability to acknowledge mistakes and limitations
3. Openness to new ideas
4. Keeping one's accomplishments and abilities in perspective
5. Relatively low self-focus
6. Appreciating diverse perspectives[9]

Humility is not just involved in how we relate to others. Dr. McMinn also describes humility's role in our relation to God (or our Higher Power), nature, self, and even information (via intellectual humility). His interpretation of the biblical text in Matthew 22 offers a way to ground us in the essence of humility:

Who asked Jesus the question, "Teacher, which is the most important commandment in the law of Moses?" (v. 36)? It was a chest-thumping linebacker, a narcissistic politician, a self-absorbed religious personality. All of these embody a me-centered approach to the world, where I am simply the best and you are not. The person asking Jesus the question was a religious expert who set out to trap Jesus, probably threatened by the crowds following Jesus.

Confronted with the smallness of petty human jealousy, Jesus answered by offering the telos of humility—a picture of what a whole, fully functioning, flourishing human being might look like. It's the one who loves God with [their] whole being and loves neighbor as self.

This is the essence of humility.[10]

Humility may not come naturally to us as helpers, especially as we battle its opposite: pride. Helpers can sometimes struggle to acknowledge their pride because their orientation to serving others often masks their self-serving motivations, even if these under-pinning motivations were instinctively adopted out of a need to protect themselves from pain and rejection. We have the knowl-edge to help, are aware of the surrounding systems, acquire the relevant skills, and more. The knowledge and skills make helpers effective but they can set us up for a massive case of pride, espe-cially when we fail to also see our vulnerability, limitations, and need for help.

So, what might it look like to practice humility?

First, recognize the areas of your life where you have honest needs and limitations, or where you need help in your own jour-ney of healing. Then confess your needs to others and invite them to come alongside you to help identify and meet those needs. This confession and invitation can be a powerful tool in helping to deconstruct pride.

Once we ask for help, we must practice *receiving* help. This may seem simple, but for helpers, the narrative that "I do the helping and others receive my help" runs deep. Receiving help from others deconstructs this narrative and helps us understand how the Sacred works through others to show us our belovedness.

As a practical example, I could easily ignore the accountability list from my doctor, described in chapter 6. In fact, though it hangs on our refrigerator door, I still ignore it from time to time. But as part of my one-day-at-a-time humility work, I regularly examine that list, take the suggestions to heart, and apply my doctor's wisdom by getting outside, limiting my email time, setting a regular bedtime, and saying no. Receiving others' support—especially among trusted loved ones and trained providers—and implementing their suggestions is not easy work. Even as I type this, I'm reminded of how stubborn my pride can be—this practice of humility is a *practice*.

Finally, the practice of humility requires us to take an honest assessment of our limitations. These can be easily ignored when we constantly focus on others' needs. I've found a regular weekly practice of assessing my schedule and to-dos helps me gain a more accurate view of my finite time and energy, acknowledge my mistakes and limitations, and keep my accomplishments and abilities in perspective alongside my priorities and values.

However you approach the practice of humility, my hope is that you regularly and seriously consider it within your journey of seeking the Sacred. You are worthy of the care you extend to so many others, and many of those around you who also bear the divine spark want to help you too. Practicing humility helps you receive their love and care as you equally extend love and care to others.

Engaging Interfaith Dialogue and Intercultural Immersion Experiences

Finally, one of the most transformative practices in helping me see the Sacred in others has been engaging in interfaith dialogue and humbly learning from other faith traditions, which has helped me appreciate the diverse ways other religious groups view, experience, and connect with the Divine. I began this practice almost by accident when I moved to Texas with my mom and my adoptive dad, who identified as Buddhist. Through conversations with my dad, I learned to look for the common threads of love despite our differences in religious belief. We never tried to proselytize or convert the other, and we always approached the conversation with humility and respect.

During my graduate program, I had the opportunity to study abroad for a few weeks in Turkey under one of my mentors, Dr. Andy Achenbaum (mentioned in chapter 1), alongside a group of students and staff. I seized the once-in-a-lifetime chance, having fallen in love with this topic of spirituality in social work and having grown familiar with Rumi's poetry. During our trip, we saw the religious diversity in the country and both heard and felt the calls to prayer. We visited historical religious sites, including the Hagia Sophia and the Blue Mosque in Istanbul, the cave churches in Cappadocia, the House of the Virgin Mary atop Mt. Koressos, and we even walked around Ephesus where the Apostle Paul preached. We toured the Topkapı Palace in Istanbul and saw diverse religious artifacts. One of the most powerful stops, though, was the Mevlâna Museum, Rumi's burial site in Konya. There, I felt the overwhelming sense of the immanent and transcendent as I walked through the rose garden beside my mentor, surrounded by people from all around the world.

During this trip, I learned that true unity is found in diversity. As a result, I returned changed. I began to look for ways to honor the religious diversity in others as I helped those whose journeys, thoughts, and experiences were different than mine. And when it came time to submit my reflection paper for the 2010 course, I wrote the following:

... the grand lesson of this course was the big picture ... [learning] that life is not about the details, data, or drama—it's about seeing beyond that to the Divine. Rather than looking closely at the details in life's tapestry (which can be beautiful), studying those details, and sticking by them for comfort, it's about taking those steps back and seeing how all the details come together to create a masterpiece ... without losing the point at which we started. We're all at different stages in this process, or a different number of steps back from the focal point of our belief system (whether the focal point is in Christianity, Judaism, Islam, Buddhism, Hinduism, or atheism). But by standing too close to our belief without allowing other beliefs to at least come into side view, of course the viewer is left thinking their religion is right and others are wrong, because without stepping back, the one they focus on is all they see!

By increasing the number of steps back we take, a wider view of the tapestry slowly comes into vision, and we begin to see others viewing the same beautiful piece before us at a different angle. By opening up, being vulnerable, allowing curiosity in about what others see, and connecting with those who stand at a different angle from the great tapestry, it creates a dialogue—the best kind—because it's pure, genuine, and innocent. By initiating this dialogue, we can let go of our tunnel vision to discover the true beauty of what's directly in front of us and, ultimately, what lies within us.

This paper closed with a portion of one of Rumi's poems—"Out beyond ideas of wrongdoing and rightdoing, there is a field. I'll meet you there."[11] Those lines were a subtle reminder that our souls are all bound for the same field, connected by the Divine. And while we may not reach this field until that moment after our last breath, it seems there's an invitation for us to move beyond dualistic thinking during our life, contemplating the Sacred connection between us and interacting with each other in a way that transcends our many differences.

Of course, traveling overseas to practice interfaith dialogue is not always feasible, and I recognize the gift of this trip during graduate school. I also recognize that there's a lot of trust, humility, and care that's required for these conversations to be helpful, healing, and honoring. Thankfully, there are several interfaith organizations, conferences, and resources we can learn from (such as the Interfaith Youth Core, Interfaith Alliance, and Parliament of the World's Religions, to name a few).[12] You might also consider listening to podcasts to hear others engage in interfaith dialogue or discuss religious beliefs you're unfamiliar with. Perhaps you could read memoirs or biographies of spiritual leaders from different faith traditions, or visit your local temple, mosque, synagogue, or church. (However, if you do visit a local faith community, please contact them in advance to ask if there are any considerations or items to bring out of cultural humility, sensitivity, and respect for their beliefs and traditions.)

The two shifts outlined in this chapter—the shift in response to seeing the Sacred in yourself and the shift toward seeing the Sacred in others—are a necessary part of this journey into Namaste Theory. They require intentional practice, including seeking the Sacred, leaning into humility, and participating in interfaith dialogue. And as you use these practices to support you in your pursuit of seeking the Sacred, you'll find yourself ready to move into the final stage: Serve.

Reflection Exercises

Reflect upon two or three people in your life who may seem very different from you, and consider how you see the image of God in them. Identify one way you can practice seeking the image of God in them this week.

Think about the roles of pride and humility in your day-to-day life. How does the slippery slope of pride show up for you as a helper? How does the practice of humility show up?

Identify a time when you engaged in interfaith dialogue or watched others engage in interfaith dialogue. What was that experience like and what did you learn from that opportunity? If this practice is new to you, consider trying one recommendation above and spend some time journaling about your experience.

CHAPTER 10

Serve

This brief lifetime is my opportunity to receive love,
deepen love, grow in love, and give love.[1]

—Fr. Henri Nouwen

On the first Sunday after the World Health Organization declared the COVID-19 outbreak a pandemic in March 2020, our congregation's lead pastor, Josh Carney, empathically and awkwardly led us through an online worship service. Nearly all faith communities shut their doors that week to protect their congregations, and while our pastor's entire sermon was heavy and humbling considering our stripped illusion of control, one point in the sermon took my breath away.

A few weeks prior, Josh had read Rev. Nadia Bolz-Weber's "Modern Beatitudes" from 2014, which was Bolz-Weber's way of blessing her congregants wherever they might be along their faith journey.[2] Inspired by her sermon and by Fred Rogers's "look for the helpers" quote mentioned in chapter 4, Josh wrote his own prayer, mindful of those who were helping on the front lines of the pandemic in different ways. The prayer was entitled "The Helpers (A Pastoral Prayer for 3-15-20)," and it was beautiful, one that I've kept close since hearing.[3] The following is a slightly abbreviated version:

The Helpers (A Pastoral Prayer for 3-15-20), by Josh Carney

Blessed are the [grocery store] workers, gas station attendants, postal carriers, and anyone who went to work so that the rest of us could buy the things we think we need.

Blessed are the doctors and nurses and health care workers who haven't slept in weeks and who expose themselves to danger so we can feel safe every day.

Blessed are the policy makers who are exhausted because they are emotionally torn by how their decision will impact all of us.

Blessed are the nerdy people who got made fun of for loving science as a kid but are doing critical research to save lives.

Blessed are the free Internet providers, Zoom chat room space creators, and anyone else who gave of their abundance so that the lonely could have community.

Blessed are those who provide food: the lunch ladies, superintendents, and politicians who fought for kids to keep eating, and the restaurant owners who are providing free meals for children.

Blessed are the opera singers, actors, dancers, and entertainers who are giving their talents away for free so that we can experience joy.

Blessed are the teachers who are worrying about that kid who they know has a hard home life.

Blessed are the burned-out stay-at-home moms and dads who are going stir crazy.

Blessed are the working parents who are now stay-at-home moms and dads because they didn't have another choice.

Blessed is the person who grabbed two gallons of milk, but put one back because there were only two left.

Blessed are those who volunteer to provide transportation for those in need and run errands for strangers.

Blessed are the fearful, for you have considered the cost and are still showing up.

Blessed are those with anxiety attacks and thoughts that everyone else considers irrational. You care deeply and it consumes you—hidden inside of that is love and we can see it.

Blessed are the pregnant, the children, the elderly, and the immunocompromised who are particularly vulnerable. Your lives are worth more than the stock market, productivity, and our lives being easy. We needed that reminder.

Blessed are the people with power who made decisions to cancel large gatherings to save lives even though they'll lose money.

Blessed are those who are enduring criticism for canceling large events because they have dared to believe in data that will not be able to prove them right if it works.

Blessed are the small business owners whose existence has been teetering for years because of [online retailers], but whose presence on one critical night provided children's Tylenol for a customer very much in need.

Blessed are the companies that are using their power and privilege to fight price gouging.

Blessed are those who are using their social media platforms to rebuke racism.

Blessed are those who have lost, are losing, or will lose. You are dust and for the first time you really know it.

Jesus blesses you.

Jesus blesses you. This blessedness, this inherent belovedness is the fuel for our service. It moves us and animates us on our journey of seeking the Sacred. And threaded through Carney's prayer is the reminder that we have unique areas of service that only we can offer as helpers. So, how can we serve from that blessedness?

Serving from Abundance

As author Sue Monk Kidd notes, there is a uniqueness within each soul, an "inner Music that plays in you as it does in no one else."[4] And as cliché as this may sound, there is no one like you in the world. No one has walked your journey, navigated your traumas and heartaches, experienced the love and joy you've experienced, obtained the exact education you have, traveled to all the same places as you, or seen all that you've seen.

More to the point, no one has experienced the divine spark within you quite like you've experienced it. What does that mean? Practically speaking, it means you not only bear the image of God within you, but you bear it in a stunningly unique way that no one else on the entire planet ever has, does, or will. (Allow that to sink in for a moment.) It means that no one can serve others quite like you can serve others.

As you connect with the divine spark as only you can, as you serve in ways unique to you, I hope you'll find a new energy, a deeper well from which to draw. I hope you'll serve from abundance, which means more than serving from a place of physical rest or excessive financial wealth. Serving from abundance means serving from the deep realization that you are unique, one of a kind, and that only you can serve in the way you can serve.[5] It also means that, even if your service efforts include licensing requirements and professional expectations, you don't have to serve in the exact same way as anyone else in your field. There is no service competition, and hustling more will not make you more important, cherished, or loved. There is nothing you could do that would make God love you more.

You are freed from hustling for your worth.

By deeply knowing your belovedness and uniqueness, you may begin to sense a profound freedom. Your imagination might run wild with ideas for helping others that only you can pull off. I hope you will stretch your idea of "service" to consider the diverse ways you are invited to serve in every interaction, each day.

Let's start with what you do throughout most of your week. If you work full time, how are you serving others in your job? Are you a barista who uses your love of art and people to create amazing latte designs that bring joy to your customers? Are you a CEO who grew up in a blue-collar home who now uses your privilege, education, and background to provide students who have fewer resources with educational opportunities? Are you a religious leader who's navigated depression, and now you use your understanding of mental illness to connect congregants to mental health care providers? Are you a first responder who uses your unparalleled capacity for empathy to offer comfort to someone who is hurting or their loved ones who are in shock? Are you a parent who experienced childhood trauma or neglect, and now you use your access to local mental health resources to equip your child with emotional intelligence? Are you a teacher who uses your love of knowledge to inspire your students?

Take a moment. Consider these questions:

- *How do you use your unique skills, experiences, and talents to serve others?*
- *How could you serve more intentionally, recognizing that those you serve are carriers of the same divine spark that's within you?*

Your life is a gift, and as you pursue Namaste Theory—seeing the divine spark in yourself and others—you can share the gift of your life with others. And as you can see, there are endless ways we can show up to serve. But don't forget, Namaste Theory is rooted in mindfully maintaining the proper speed even as we serve. Put another way, the most effective and healthiest helpers remember they each have a finite amount of time, energy, and resources.

Trying to do everything for everyone all of the time will invariably spread you thin, deplete you of the abundance from which you're serving, strap your foot to the accelerator again, and press your foot down hard. And as you serve from a place of depletion, it will reengage the old compulsive hustling for your worth. The result? Acts of service will become fractured at best, harmful at worst.

And that brings me back to the core of Namaste Theory. Remember, as you serve others, recognizing the divine spark within them, you must not lose sight of recognizing and serving the divine spark in your own soul. To be clear, serving your soul is not the same as serving your ego, unhealthy attachments, pride, programs for happiness, or lies of identity. It's about humbly discerning your innermost needs and meeting them to the best of your ability. After all, we cannot give to others what we don't give ourselves, whether it's rest, presence, trust, kindness, empathy, joy, gentleness, peace, or love. We cannot draw water from an empty well. We must recognize our human limitations.

As I've demonstrated in this book, this process of recognizing my limitations has not been easy, and I still wrestle with it. I've followed every signpost, signal, and systemic message that said *keep going*. I've pushed forward for "noble" reasons (according to others, that is), despite being exhausted. My ego enjoyed the praise for all I was juggling, the admiration for being some kind of superhuman, and the accolades I've earned along the way. And the scary thing is, I bought the lie that this was what God wanted, that I was partnering with God through my hustling. I thought I was making God and those around me happy, all the while making myself and my family miserable. I thought I was stewarding my energy, resources, and time for others, when in reality I was hustling for my self-worth. This is not to negate seasons when I truly felt aligned with that inner Music that Sue Monk Kidd writes about, but to humbly admit there have been times when I've incorrectly chosen busy over being, hurrying over healing, and proving over presence as I hustled for my worth.

I've come to realize that God does not delight in our burnout, and we earn *zero* badges of honor, gold stars, or bonus points for burning out. In fact, without shaming us, I imagine God grieves while watching us burn out, wishing we would steward the gift of our life by learning to discern what is ours to do, one moment at a time—nothing more and nothing less. We're invited to recognize the honest and humbling limitations of our humanity, and create space for God to be God, particularly as it relates to the work that's beyond our capacity.

Even Jesus of Nazareth didn't constantly offer every ounce of energy to others. He didn't heal every person. He didn't serve himself into exhaustion and didn't glorify burnout while pursuing productivity and efficiency. Instead, he was fully present, and both before and after intense moments of service, he retreated. For example, he retreated after the feeding of 5,000 (Matthew 14:22–23) and before choosing his twelve apostles (Luke 6:12). He went away to pray. He rested. He slept. He ate. He *received* love from God. He recharged so he could serve out of a place of abundance, doing the work that was specifically his to do.

This realization fundamentally shifted my understanding of serving others as a helper. If my faith leads me to believe Jesus rested throughout his service, then why shouldn't I take rest very seriously? Why shouldn't I weave rest into my own life, even (and especially) in the middle of very busy seasons of service or as I'm learning new ways to serve? And why shouldn't I advocate for and encourage other helpers to experience the necessity of rest too?

So, how do we create practices that support us as we discern service opportunities? How can we protect our souls as we move into service so everything we do flows from a place of abundance—of knowing our inherent worth—instead of a place of burnout?

Practices to Help Us Serve

In chapter 1, we briefly touched on a few different models describing our spiritual growth and development. One of those included Dr. James Fowler's stages of faith, and although I didn't cover the details of each stage, I will highlight the final stage he proposes: universalizing faith.[6] Those in this stage live counter to their culture. They selflessly serve from a place of unconditional love and without many real worries or doubts. They view everyone as part of a universal family, with a universal human vocation, and often dedicate their lives to service. And by "everyone," I mean "everyone, including yourself."

As we awaken to the Sacred within and see it in others, it's as though we're naturally drawn to serve the image of God within and all around us in whatever way our divine spark guides us. This is true whether we're helping others in our professions, through hobbies or community service projects, or through our day-to-day interactions with family members, loved ones, and ourselves. With careful intention and gentle attention, we must nurture the Sacred within us as we continue to serve those around us.

Many of the previous chapters' practices helped position us to see the Sacred and discern what is ours to do, what we have capacity for, and how to set appropriate boundaries. Most importantly, these practices helped us learn to humbly and nonjudgmentally monitor our motivations, assess our potential risk of projecting our pain onto others, or recognize our tendencies to hustle for an illusion of worth through our service.

As we navigate this stage of the journey, the following practices can help cultivate and deepen a sense of groundedness within ourselves to hold the necessary space for others as we serve.

Journaling

Hidden in the corner of my closet is a stack of journals that go back to when I was ten years old. However, it wasn't until around 2008 that I began journaling on a weekly basis as a way of slowing my thinking for the purposes of self-discovery and practicing discernment. Throughout the week, it felt as though I was holding emotions, experiences, and events (my own and others') in my heart, and I needed an unfiltered space to release all I had taken in.

In chapter 8, I highlighted the practice of writing, but journaling holds a different purpose for me. Namely, journaling is the space where I can set down all I've been carrying through the week, like setting down a tray filled with items. Without this practice, the threads of emotion within my heart feel so tightly woven together, making it difficult to discern where one emotion begins and another ends. And it's not just my emotions hidden within. At times, I'll even catch myself carrying others' emotions that I've held space for during a recent conversation—a friend's grief, a colleague's frustration, a loved one's joy. Oftentimes and unknowingly, these emotions stick with me throughout the week. Plus, my thoughts and physical sensations regularly get tangled in the emotions too. (Perhaps you have also felt this way?) But by setting aside at least one window per week to slowly, gently, and carefully unwrap each of those threads of emotions, thoughts, and sensations in my journal, I can discern which are mine to carry, which I need to tend to or let go, which I need to learn from, and which are simply distractions. It's a process that gives me a clearer view of my inner landscape and allows me to tend to the Sacred within me as I serve others.

Of course, there are weeks (or even certain days) when I don't protect time for this practice, and my emotional landscape becomes overgrown. I begin to feel worn out. But when I return to my journaling practice, when I process my emotions, acknowledge my thoughts, honor my sensations, and set down what isn't mine to continually carry, things seem to lighten.

Maybe you don't journal, but the process sounds intriguing. How do you begin? Personally, I set aside an hour or so once a week (usually Sunday morning or afternoon) and write out in a notebook whatever emotions, thoughts, or sensations arise, pausing as often as needed to tune in. I might journal about an interaction with a loved one, a national event, a sticky emotion I can't shake, or deep inner nudges calling me to pay attention. I breathe deeply and begin to free-write what I'm carrying within me, reaching deep, regarding nothing as off limits. I excavate as much as I can, not only to free myself from carrying it but to discover what else might be deeper beneath the surface. As I unwind all that is within me, tears often surface, but so does grace, remembering I am doing the best I can in light of all I'm carrying. Through journaling, I often become aware of exactly how much I *have* been carrying without realizing it.

By engaging in this regular practice, I'm better able to discern what is mine to set down or to carry, ultimately helping me clarify what is mine to do as I serve. Pick up a journal and a pen. See if the same is true for you.

Mental Health Care and Therapy

Especially recognizing the intersection of spirituality and mental health, the journey of seeking the Sacred moves us toward spiritual and emotional healing. Ideally, it motivates us to prioritize cultivating a healthy space to house the divine spark within us. To that end, I cannot overemphasize the value of having a well-trained, licensed mental health care provider who regularly reflects the image of God within you and who continually invites you into a place of wholeness and healing.

As you might remember from chapter 2, over 80 percent of us will experience a mental health struggle by young adulthood or middle age.[7] This means very few of us will navigate life without at least one mental health struggle at some point. In the same way we routinely see doctors or dentists for preventative physical or dental care, why not schedule regular mental health checkups for the stressors, anxieties, and traumas we experience along the way? If we're able to, these checkups can help to build the rapport we need with a trusted provider before we find ourselves in crisis.

Receiving mental health care and therapy can also help us awaken to and slow our speed (chapters 4 and 5), receive support from others (chapter 6), practice nonjudgmental self-observation (chapter 7), recognize our attachments to the programs for happiness and how they motivate our behaviors (chapter 8), and support our practice of humility (chapter 9). Put another way, therapeutic services are critical to living into these stages of seeking the Sacred.

Of any practices outlined in this book, this is the one I would most elevate and strongly encourage fellow helpers to explore, with centering prayer as a very close second. (Goodness, could you imagine the healing in the world if all helpers were doing their inner work with a trusted, licensed mental health care provider?) Still, as a social worker, I'm mindful there are many barriers to receiving mental health care support. There are financial barriers, proximity and location limitations, technological restrictions, shame or stigma relating to mental illness and treatment, and more. Some of these may be more difficult to overcome, while others may be alleviated with some local support. For example, the 2-1-1 helpline (or www.211.org), is one way to connect with local resources, including available mental health services in your community. You can also ask your primary care doctor for a referral or visit the resources in the back of the book to help you find a local therapist.

Consider finding a clinically trained mental health care provider in your area, such as a licensed social worker, psychologist, professional counselor, marriage and family therapist, or psychiatrist. Pick up the phone and schedule an appointment to begin healing your inner landscape, the place where you tend to your own divine spark. (You can always cancel the appointment if you change your mind.) And if this feels out of reach financially, call a therapist anyway. Many have programs and sliding-scale fees to assist those who need financial assistance. If you have health insurance, you can also contact your insurance company for support in finding a provider, or if your company has an employee assistance program, it may offer free or discounted counseling services.

Normalize therapy in your life and see it as part of the way you serve others by serving your own soul. Your friends, family members, colleagues, and those you help will thank you for it.

Rest and Retreats

To combat Nouwen's lies of identity (see chapter 8)—that we are what we have, what we do, or what others say or think about us—particularly in the ways we serve others, we need to step out of the everyday busyness and remember our belovedness. This will help us to serve from a place of abundance. Aside from a regular centering prayer practice, I have found no better way to remember my identity as the Beloved than cultivating intentional rest beyond my weekly Sabbath day.

Over the last few years, I've recognized the invaluable gift of going away on retreats. As Ruth Haley Barton explains in her book *Invitation to Retreat*, "Retreat in the context of the spiritual life is an *extended time apart* for the purpose of being with God and giving God our full and undivided attention." Through understanding retreat as a "strategic withdrawal" and exploring this idea of retreat throughout her book, Barton explains, "We will hear God's invitation to *rest* and learn what we must *relinquish* in order to do that. We will experience *rhythms* that *replenish* us—body, mind, and soul. We will practice *recognizing* and *responding* to the presence of God through discernment, and *recalibrate* based on what God is saying to our souls. We will feel ourselves drawn to *reengage* our lives in the company of others from a more rested place and establish regular patterns of *returning* and *resting* in God."[8]

Separating from the familiar, day-to-day activities for a window of intentional retreat helps me reconnect with the divine spark within me, refill my well, and reestablish groundedness, knowing that I am loved and enough as I am. Being on retreat reconnects me with a much bigger story than the one my calendar and to-do list tells. In fact, being on retreat helps me lean into a simple but powerful prayer: "God help me see my life as you see it and myself in it as you see me."[9]

Practically speaking, retreats can be as short as an afternoon at a park, a day or two at a nearby retreat center or monastery, or a week or longer. They also serve as an invitation to get away from distracting social media, emails, texts, and calendar notifications. And especially in the case of silent retreats, they can invite us into a very deep state of *being*.

Regardless of the length or format of your retreat, be intentional and carve out the extended time away that your soul needs, even just once a year. Step away from the routine, unplug, and tend to your inner space. If you give in to the practice, you'll find yourself recharged and recentered as you return to your helper roles.

Stand in Solidarity with Helpers

Finally, without any strings attached, provide the same support to a fellow helper you might want to receive. How? Stand in solidarity with them.

There are many ways of standing in solidarity with other helpers. You might financially support a fellow helper's organization, helping to alleviate their financial worry or stress. You might spend a Saturday covering a fellow helper's shift at a local nonprofit agency so they can have a retreat day. Maybe you volunteer to read to an elementary classroom monthly, giving the teacher a short break. Maybe you amplify the good work of local agencies in your community by sharing their links and resources. Maybe you watch your single neighbor's kids for a couple of hours in order to give them a break.

Supporting a fellow helper could also look like sending random thank-you notes just because you see the efforts of your fellow helpers and you want to encourage them. Perhaps it means sitting in prayer for a few minutes a day, holding space and courageously allowing your heart to be broken open by the incredible suffering in this world as you pray for those who tend to it. And as you do all of this, remember, the goal is to serve the Sacred in your fellow helper just as you serve the Sacred in yourself.

Serving Others, Serving Our Soul

Recall Carney's prayer at the beginning of this chapter. Do you see yourself in it? Read it again, recognizing the deep truths: you are blessed and beloved, there is help only you can offer, and you must tend to that work. Recognize this truth too: if you do not tend to and care for your whole self, if you do not create conditions for healthy service, you'll be in danger of burning out and harming others despite your intentions to help.

You are an intricate part of this world, and by healing what's within, by remembering your identity as the Beloved, you will help to heal the world. You are worth caring for as you care for others. You are worth serving as you serve others. Do not lose sight of this truth. By remembering it, you're setting yourself up for a lifetime of abundant service.

Reflection Exercises

Name a form of serving others or your own soul that, when you're engaged in it, time stands still, you feel fully alive, or it seems as though your well is filled with more energy, joy, and love. Spend some time reflecting upon this form of service and what about it is so fulfilling to you.

Reflect upon how you're serving others in your day-to-day life, whether it's at work, home, or in the community. Journal for twenty minutes, reflecting on whether these acts come from a place of abundance or whether they feel depleting. Get curious.

Pick one of the practices in this chapter to try this week. Consider asking your medical doctor for a referral to a mental health care provider. Perhaps you identify a nearby retreat center and schedule an overnight retreat. Simply pick up a pen and journal and start writing. What is one way you can serve and support your soul as you serve others?

PART III

"So What?"

Cultivating a Practice of Seeking and Serving the Sacred for the Journey Ahead

CHAPTER 11

Seek and Serve the Sacred

Spiritual seekers let their light shine so that others may see not only to give service by example but also to constantly remind themselves that spirituality is most gloriously embodied in our actions—our habits of being.[1]

—bell hooks

In my years of teaching research and statistics courses, I've learned an important lesson. If I don't ask students "So what?" by the end of class and invite them to reflect upon the content we've covered, they'll leave class without knowing how to apply the material. They will check the attendance box, of course, and perhaps will have even listened and learned something new, but without identifying *why* it matters to them—their unique "So what?"—they will not be transformed by the material.

More to the point, without allowing my students to answer "So what?" I've missed an important opportunity as a helper, specifically as an educator. I've failed to usher them into a deeper understanding of why the material matters and why we spent hours covering it. In so doing, I've failed to empower them to connect the course content with the tools they need in their own lives as helpers.

As a professor training the next generation of critical thinkers in social work, I want my students to get to the heart of what matters in the content. I also want them to get in the habit of asking "So what?" time and time again in their own lives. The same is true for this book and for you.

Transformational Education

At Baylor University, there are four distinct pillars that have and continue to shape the university: the Christian educational environment; transformational education; high-quality and impactful research and scholarship; and human performance in the arts and athletics.[2] It's the second pillar—transformational education—that really drew me to the university. Baylor describes a transformational education as "one in which students develop their leadership potential, explore their faith and beliefs, increase their desire for wisdom, and prepare for service in a diverse and interconnected global society."[3] Although I wrote about the importance of this pillar in my annual tenure review materials, it wasn't until after going through this research that I came to realize we cannot offer transformational education if we're unwilling to be transformed ourselves.[4]

Without a shadow of a doubt, I have been fundamentally transformed by my research over the last thirteen years, as well as my work around developing and applying Namaste Theory, including these seven stages of seeking the Sacred. It's transformed the ways I approach each student, seeing them more clearly as carriers of the divine spark. It's transformed the way I engage my faculty colleagues, celebrating with them in their success and commiserating with them in their distress. It's changed the way I serve in the community, too, as I try to serve only out of abundance. It's changed the way I seek to show up and remain present to my partner and kids, even after difficult days, recognizing that whatever isn't transformed within me will be transmitted to those closest to me. And it's changed the way I practice self-care, recognizing I am worth caring for and tending to the gift of my precious and sacred life, including my physical health, mental and emotional health, relationships, and spiritual journey.

Still, in all humility and as long as I'm breathing, I know I'll struggle to practice Namaste Theory and these stages of seeking the Sacred because I'm human. I'll be tempted to inch my foot toward the accelerator, trying to do more and move faster in an effort to earn approval and avoid rejection. I may even be tempted to use some of the helpful practices noted in this book as another form of performative hustling if I'm not choosing them with intention. I'm sure I'll become unsteady, unable to see the Sacred within me with a nonjudgmental lovingkindness. I'm positive my loved ones will share how my struggles to see the Sacred impact them. Namaste Theory, including these seven stages to see the Sacred within myself and in the world around me, will offer me the reminders to reconnect with my inner divine spark and serve from knowing my inherent belovedness.

This brings me to our "So what?"

As much as I wish everyone on this journey of seeking the Sacred could gather in a classroom and share their own unique insights, we can't. So I invite you to pause for a moment and write your own sacred insights. Take as much space and time as you need, either writing in the space below or in a journal. By writing it down, you'll be less likely to forget.

So, what's *your* unique *aha*, the thought, awareness, or awakening you didn't have before reading this book? What understandings or insights have deepened through reading it? Write them below.

_____

_____

_____

_____

Even though we can't gather in a room to share our insights,
social media allows us to exchange ideas and takeaways with
one another. There is no pressure to participate or share your
insights, but if you choose to, you're welcome to do so on social
media using the hashtag #TheSoulOfTheHelper.

Now that you've identified your unique insights, writing what feels most true for you after reading this book, I want to offer my own "So what?" answers. And even if these answers are different from your own unique insights, I hope you'll spend time contemplating them.

First, let's circle back to some of A. K. Krishna Nambiar's words from chapter 3 and expand the quote slightly regarding this practice of folding our hands as a symbol of combining matter and spirit with Namaste:

Namaste recognises two forces that have ever existed in this world and suggests an effort on our part to bring these forces together in human relations. What are these two forces behind *Namaste*? They are Matter and Spirit.

. . . This gesture is an expression of humility: "I recognise God in you." If a human relationship begins with this feeling, can there be any room for crookedness and cunning in our dealings with each other? [HKO note: including our desire and efforts to help] . . .

. . . When [*Namaste*] is extended to human beings it recognises the divinity in [humans] and thus [their] form is also recognised as the moving temple of God. . . .

When we fold our hands for *Namaste*, this philosophy, symbolised by our ten fingers of both hands, reminds us to think and act correctly. . . . In this manner, feeling and action become integrated in *Namaste*. As this produces a state of introspection, we become capable of thinking of the source of existence that is within every one of us and in the universe.

Namaste initiates us into the mysteries of the inner world because in its true spirit we can observe by our inner awareness that the world within us is limitless. . . .

. . . *Namaste* in its true spirit helps our ego to surrender to the goal of our faith. . . . *Namaste* helps us to break all the barriers in us and to become humble. This in turn makes us work as an instrument of God in the spiritual or social fields of our activities. . . .

Though *Namaste* can be nourished and grown in any religious atmosphere, it ultimately helps us to transcend all limitations including the religious denomination under which we developed it. This is because *Namaste* aims at an integrated personality where heart and head are united in oneness. Therefore, *Namaste* removes all barriers that divide [human] and [human] and unites [humankind] in faith and wisdom. Ultimately, it is the faith and wisdom that will triumph over any sectarian practices in religions and finally religions themselves. And what we are in its evolutionary process actually experiencing in our development and progress through *Namaste* is knowledge. When this knowledge grows in faith, it becomes wisdom and this is the goal of the simple *Namaste* greeting and therefore it is equally applicable to everybody alike, irrespective of caste, creed, colour or nationality.

Once matter and spirit are integrated in a personality, *Namaste* helps to reveal love.[5]

Recognizing the Sacred within ourselves and others not only ushers us into a humble surrender, but as we see and know this truth, we can "work as an instrument of God in the spiritual or

social fields of our activities."[6] Isn't this what so many of us as helpers want as we go out and serve others?

Our work as instruments of God cannot be primarily motivated by outer pressures, structures, or systems. It should not
be influenced by our own ego or unhealthy attachments either.
Instead, when we practice Namaste—when we pursue a deep, infinite, integrated "spirit and matter" desire to bring forward healing
and wholeness in ourselves and in the world around us—we can
better discern what is truly ours to do. And then we can go do it to
the best of our ability.

The risk of not tuning in to the Sacred within and carefully
tending to it is far too urgent for us as helpers. Not only do we
miss out on our one, precious, and sacred life, but we also risk
imposing our own attachments to security and survival, affection
and esteem, and power and control onto others in the name of
helping. Further, we run the imminent risk of burnout as we chase
these illusive programs for happiness that will never satisfy us in
the ways the Sacred within will. And if we continue to operate at a
breakneck speed through these unpromised days we're given,
never practicing the stillness needed to fully see or honor the
Sacred within ourselves, my fear is that we won't be able to fully
see or honor the Sacred within others.

More simply put in bullet list fashion:

- If we're burned out as helpers, we cannot see the Sacred
  within and will miss it in those within our care.
- If we're not connected with our inherent belovedness, we
  will risk imposing our broken need for security and
  survival, affection and esteem, and power and control onto
  others through our hustling to earn these programs for
  happiness.

- If we neglect seeing, honoring, and loving the image of God within ourselves, we will fail to fully see, honor, and love the image of God within our neighbors.

In light of these reflections, there are three primary answers to "So what?" to offer. I hope you'll carry these answers with you as you close this book and continue on your own journey through the seven stages of seeking the Sacred.

1. You bear the image of God, the divine spark within.

You were created by Love out of love in order to love. Your identity is the Beloved and you are to remember this and remind others of their belovedness. Jesus reminds us of this in his teaching on the greatest commandment in Matthew 22:37–39 (NIV) (again, echoed in Mark 12:29–31, Luke 10:27, and John 13:34, amplifying the importance of this message). He says we're to "'Love the Lord your God with all your heart and with all your soul and with all your mind.' This is the first and greatest commandment. And the second is like it: 'Love your neighbor as yourself.'"

Those of us who look to Jesus as our guide are instructed to love God, our neighbor, *and* ourselves (although this teaching to love one another traces back to Leviticus 19:18 and is generally echoed in many other religious traditions). And if you consider the commandment critically, the requirement to love our neighbors *as ourselves* requires us to first love ourselves. Completely. Without condition or any strings attached.

Unfortunately, I'm afraid loving ourselves and honoring the image of God within ourselves is rarely woven into the fabric of the religious messaging we receive. In fact, I imagine many of us have heard more messages about how sinful, bad, wrong, dirty, small, and unworthy we are than messages about how we are completely and wholly loved, just as we are. And if we adopt these negative messages about ourselves, can we truly love our neighbors? Again, when I speak of loving ourselves, I'm not referring to loving our egos or accomplishments, but rather, loving ourselves as we are, as we were created, as image bearers of God.

2. Seeking the Sacred within helps you to recognize and honor it in others.

Tuning into your belovedness and seeing the Sacred within yourself will awaken you to see the Sacred in others. As you recognize this divine spark in yourself—a gift that you did nothing to earn or achieve—you'll come to realize that every human being carries the same infinite, inherent worth.

Recognizing the Sacred in those we're helping should reorient us. It should inspire us to tend to our own inner landscape, to care for, heal, and integrate what's within so we can serve God fully as we serve others. That is, after all, the aim of Namaste Theory—allowing the Sacred within me to honor the Sacred within others, particularly through service.

3. We must explore and tend to our inner landscape so we can tend to the world around us.

If we don't tend to our inner wounds, unheralded traumas, and deep heartache, we'll pass pain onto others. The traumatic childhood memories that occasionally resurface, the unfortunate news from a boss, the cutting words from a partner, the worry from rising medical bills, the increasing demands at work, the pain and shame inflicted by a religious community, the death of a loved one—these inner wounds can run deep. If we try to stuff, avoid, or move past the emotions of those experiences without doing the necessary work of courageously sitting with and feeling them in order to heal them, they will burrow deep within our heart, mind, and body, only causing more pain. Your inner healing matters, because as you heal the wound within, you heal the world around you. Your inner healing counts as part of our global healing.

As helpers navigating these seven stages of seeking the Sacred, we must explore and move toward healing our inner wounds so we do not unintentionally pass them along to others, including our loved ones and those we serve. And, to the best of our ability, we must create and honor the boundaries needed to guard our hearts from receiving the pain others project onto us, whether they realize it or not. We must also remember that we can deeply empathize with others while discerning what is ours to do and remaining vigilant to guard against the risks of burnout.

A Critical Call for Helpers

Every interaction with others is an invitation to allow the Sacred in us to see and serve the Sacred in them. To work for the healing of others as we work toward our own healing. To awaken to and be humbled by the infinite mystery around and within us.

We will not always get it right, but still, as helpers we can try our best to practice seeking the Sacred within ourselves and others, holding space for God to do what only God can do through each of us as we follow the divine spark into the fields of our work. The risk is far too great to continue serving in any other way.

As we awaken to the Sacred within and around us, it's important to note this is not a one-and-done process. It is a humbling, never-ending journey, so long as we have breath in our lungs. Returning to Seth Haines's quote in chapter 7, "Waking gives way to waking, which gives way to waking, which gives way to waking."[7] In other words, our journey toward seeing and serving the Sacred is a continuous, unfolding, rediscovering, course-correcting, re-membering invitation from God to discover and integrate the Sacred within as we navigate this life and serve others.

What an exciting invitation, indeed!

How we navigate this life and serve others will vary based on so many layers of intersectionality. Although I follow my humble understanding of one Jewish, Middle Eastern man's journey and believe he stands apart from the rest of humanity, I also recognize Jesus invited all of us on this journey when he said, "The kingdom of God is within you" (Luke 17:21, KJV), and quite simply, "This is my command: Love each other." (John 15:17, NIV). And again, this invitation is echoed within other faith traditions alongside the subtle (and not so subtle) calls for us to wake up to the Divine within. For example, Jewish theologian and philosopher Rabbi Abraham Joshua Heschel "believed that when one understands the spark of the divine that is within each person, [they] cannot harbor hatred for fellow human beings."[8] How beautifully this runs parallel to Jesus's commandments and A. K. Krishna Nambiar's teachings on Namaste!

A Final Reminder to Serve the Sacred

Before the closing invitation, take a moment. Breathe deeply. Be present to the emotions, sensations, and insights you're carrying, including your answers to the question "So what?"

As I said in the opening intention of this book, "The ways you care for others is holy, sacred work. You bring healing to so many in the good work you do. Regardless of whether you see it, you are birthing beauty, love, goodness, and wholeness into the world. As a fellow human being, parent, teacher, loved one, and helper—thank you."

Fellow helper, you are a gift and your presence matters, aside from the good, healing, helpful things you do. The ways you are uniquely created to love and serve during your brief lifetime are precious indeed, however these show up through your presence among us. As Nouwen wrote, "service is an expression of the search for God and not just of the desire to bring about individual or social change."[9]

You are worth the process of waking up to the gift of your life and serving in whatever way the image of God within you is trying to make Itself known to you and to the rest of humanity. I hope you'll listen, pay attention, and offer what is only yours to offer in the ways you love and serve during your brief lifetime.

A Wholehearted Invitation and Benediction

Dear reader, may you *receive* this moment, this book, and these words as an invitation to seek the Sacred within as you help and serve the Sacred in others. May you return to this book as often as you need to along your holy and sacred journey. May you be reminded of your infinite and inherent value. May you tend to your own spiritual development and mental health care, becoming deeply grounded and comfortable with your inner landscape to the best of your ability. May you remember that in doing this inner work, you may be surprised by the unexpected ways in which you're inviting others to engage in their own spiritual development and wholistic healing process. May you remember that prioritizing your healing makes way for your unique service and the ways in which only you can bring healing to the world. May you trust that your inner healing counts as part of our global healing.

Above all else, I hope and pray that you see your life as a precious and holy gift. You have skills and knowledge and empathy and experiences that are unique to *you*. There is work that is *yours* to do within each unpromised day. Serve the Sacred in yourself and others as you tend to that work. See what happens as you do, dearly beloved.

Finally, I pray that you may receive these same words from the Divine that I did in the center of the labyrinth in 2018, weaving them into the fabric of your journey as a fellow helper too:

"Wake up. . . . I made you, child. I created you and I love you. You don't need to do anything for that love—it's here. I could not love you any more. I could not love you any less. I love you as you are."

May we love others in this same way, living into this call to love our neighbors *as ourselves.*

May it be so.

Namaste.

NOTES

Introduction

1. Kenneth I. Pargament, *Spiritually Integrated Psychotherapy: Understanding and Addressing the Sacred* (Guilford Press, 2007).

2. Edward P. Shafranske and H. Newton Malony, "Clinical Psychologists' Religious and Spiritual Orientations and Their Practice of Psychotherapy," *Psychotherapy* 27, no. 1 (1990): 72–78; Rachel M. Shafer et al., "Training and Education in Religion/Spirituality within APA-Accredited Clinical Psychology Programs: 8 Years Later," *Journal of Religion and Health* 50, no. 2 (2011): 232–239.

3. Holly K. Oxhandler, Google Scholar profile, accessed August 27, 2021, https://scholar.google.com/citations?user=t9JvHXoAAAAJ.

4. Center for Action and Contemplation, Living School, accessed August 27, 2021, https://cac.org/living-school/living-school-welcome.

5. Dr. Ken Pargament has also written about sacred moments in psychotherapy in his 2007 book mentioned above. See also Kenneth I. Pargament et al., "Sacred Moments in Psychotherapy from the Perspectives of Mental Health Providers and Clients: Prevalence, Predictors, and Consequences," *Spirituality in Clinical Practice* 1, no. 4 (2014): 248–262.

6. Melinda A. Stanley et al., "Lay Persons Can Deliver Effective Cognitive Behavioral Therapy for Older Adults with Generalized Anxiety Disorder: A Randomized Trial," *Depression and Anxiety* 31, no. 5 (2014): 391–401. See also Cynthia Kraus-Schuman et al.,

"Enabling Lay Providers to Conduct CBT for Older Adults: Key Steps for Expanding Treatment Capacity," *Translational Behavioral Medicine* 5, no. 3 (2015): 247–253.

7. Melinda A. Stanley et al., "Older Adults' Preferences for Religion/ Spirituality in Treatment for Anxiety and Depression," *Aging and Mental Health* 15, no. 3 (2011): 334–343.

8. Substance Abuse and Mental Health Services Administration, *Behavioral Health, United States, 2012*, https://www.store.samhsa .gov/product/Behavioral-Health-United-States-2012/SMA13 -4797.

9. Holly K. Oxhandler, "Advancing the Integration of Religion and Spirituality in Mental Health Care: Measurement and Current Implementation" (PhD diss., University of Houston, 2014), UH Electronic Theses and Dissertations, https://uh-ir.tdl.org/handle /10657/3647.

10. A. K. Krishna Nambiar, *Namaste: Its Philosophy and Significance in Indian Culture* (Spiritual India Publishing House, 1979), 2.

11. Due to the increased popular use of the word *namaste*, many interpretations of it have evolved. In this book, I try to humbly lean on what I've learned from Nambiar's writing within the cultural origins of this word. Psychologist Dr. Thomas G. Plante also describes namaste using the same general interpretations I had come across: "Namaste: It's Not Just for Those from the East," *Psychology Today*, November 10, 2010, https://www.psychologytoday.com/us/blog/do -the-right-thing/201011/namaste-its-not-just-those-the-east. Others have written about their interpretation, including this article on Deepak Chopra's website: Karson McGinley, "The Meaning of Namasté," August 25, 2019, https://chopra.com/articles/learn -the-meaning-of-namaste. Additionally, two articles on NPR's website describe it as a simple greeting: Kumari Devarajan, "How 'Namaste' Flew Away from Us," January 17, 2020, https://www.npr .org/sections/codeswitch/2020/01/17/406246770/how-namaste

-flew-away-from-us; Deepak Singh, "A Ga. School Bans the Greeting 'Namaste.' Do They Know What It Means?" July 26, 2015, https://www.npr.org/sections/goatsandsoda/2015/07/26/42596 8146/whats-in-a-namaste-depends-if-you-live-in-india-or-the-u-s. See also note 11 in chapter 3.

12. Holly K. Oxhandler, "Namaste Theory: A Quantitative Grounded Theory on Religion and Spirituality in Mental Health Treatment," *Religions* 8 (2017): 168.

Chapter 1

1. Richard Rohr, *Everything Belongs: The Gift of Contemplative Prayer* (Crossroad, 2003), 143.

2. Kenneth I. Pargament, *Spiritually Integrated Psychotherapy: Understanding and Addressing the Sacred* (Guilford Press, 2007), 32.

3. Richard Rohr, Center for Action and Contemplation, Sermon on the Mount: Week 1, "Discovering Our Inner Divine Spark," January 29, 2018, https://cac.org/discovering-inner-divine-spark-2018-01-29. This reflection not only echoes my cognitive understanding of the sacred spark from earlier readings and conversations with a mentor, but my experiential understanding of it that's later described in this book.

4. Edward R. Canda, Leola Dyrud Furman, and Hwi-Ja Canda, *Spiritual Diversity in Social Work Practice: The Heart of Helping*, 3rd ed. (Oxford University Press, 2019), 77.

5. James W. Fowler, *Stages of Faith: The Psychology of Human Development and the Quest for Meaning* (HarperOne, 1981), 91.

6. Pew Research Center, 2015, "Religious Landscape Study: Importance of Religion in One's Life," https://www.pewforum.org/religious-landscape-study/importance-of-religion-in-ones-life; "Religious Landscape Study: Religions," https://www.pewforum.org/religious-landscape-study.

7. Pew Research Center, "Chapter 2: Religious Switching and Inter-marriage," May 12, 2015, https://www.pewforum.org/2015/05/12 /chapter-2-religious-switching-and-intermarriage.

8. Michael Davern et al., General social surveys, 1972–2018 cumulative file, National Opinion Research Center, University of Chicago, 2019, https://gss.norc.org. Spiritual: https://gssdataexplorer.norc .org/variables/2121/vshow. Religious: https://gssdataexplorer.norc .org/variables/2120/vshow.

9. Pew Research Center, 2015, "Belief in God," https://www.pewforum .org/religious-landscape-study/belief-in-god; "Belief in Heaven," https://www.pewforum.org/religious-landscape-study/belief-in -heaven.

10. Pew Research Center, 2015, "Frequency of Feeling Spiritual Peace and Wellbeing," https://www.pewforum.org/religious-landscape -study/frequency-of-feeling-spiritual-peace-and-wellbeing; "Frequency of Feeling Wonder About the Universe," https://www .pewforum.org/religious-landscape-study/frequency-of-feeling -wonder-about-the-universe.

11. Pew Research Center, 2015, "Attendance at Religious Services," https://www.pewforum.org/religious-landscape-study/attendance -at-religious-services; "Frequency of Prayer," https://www.pewforum .org/religious-landscape-study/frequency-of-prayer; "Frequency of Reading Scripture," https://www.pewforum.org/religious-landscape -study/frequency-of-reading-scripture; "Frequency of Meditation," https://www.pewforum.org/religious-landscape-study/frequency -of-meditation.

12. Pew Research Center, "The Unaffiliated," 2015, https://www .pewforum.org/religious-landscape-study/religious-tradition /unaffiliated-religious-nones.

13. Fowler, *Stages of Faith*; Ken Wilber, "Introduction to the Integral Approach (and the AQAL Map)," 2006, http://www.kenwilber.com /Writings/PDF/IntroductiontotheIntegralApproach_GENERAL

_2005_NN.pdf; Mark E. Koltko-Rivera, "Rediscovering the Later Version of Maslow's Hierarchy of Needs: Self-transcendence and Opportunities for Theory, Research, and Unification," *Review of General Psychology* 10, no. 4 (2006): 302–317; Phileena Heuertz, *Pilgrimage of a Soul: Contemplative Spirituality for the Active Life* (InterVarsity Press, 2017).

14. Fowler, *Stages of Faith.*
15. Heuertz, *Pilgrimage of a Soul*, 24.
16. Heuertz, *Pilgrimage of a Soul*, 181.

Chapter 2

1. Brené Brown, *The Gifts of Imperfection: Let Go of Who You Think You're Supposed to Be and Embrace Who You Are* (Hazelden, 2010), 6.
2. Alcoholics Anonymous, *The Twelve Steps of Alcoholics Anonymous*, https://www.aa.org/assets/en_US/smf-121_en.pdf.
3. William Copeland et al., "Cumulative Prevalence of Psychiatric Disorders by Young Adulthood: A Prospective Cohort Analysis from the Great Smoky Mountains Study," *Journal of the American Academy of Child and Adolescent Psychiatry* 50, no. 3 (2011): 252–261; Jonathan D. Schaefer et al., "Enduring Mental Health: Prevalence and Prediction," *Journal of Abnormal Psychology* 126, no. 2 (2017): 212–224.
4. National Alliance on Mental Illness, "Mental Health by the Numbers," March 2021, https://www.nami.org/mhstats.
5. Richard Rohr, "Suffering: Week 1, Transforming Pain," October 17, 2018, https://cac.org/transforming-pain-2018-10-17.
6. *Psychology Today*, "Cognitive Behavioral Therapy," https://www.psychologytoday.com/us/therapy-types/cognitive-behavioral-therapy. "Eye Movement Desensitization and Reprocessing Therapy," https://www.psychologytoday.com/us/therapy-types/eye-movement-desensitization-and-reprocessing-therapy. "Acceptance

and Commitment Therapy," https://www.psychologytoday.com /us/therapy-types/acceptance-and-commitment-therapy. "Dialecti-cal Behavior Therapy," https://www.psychologytoday.com/us /therapy-types/dialectical-behavior-therapy.

7. National Alliance on Mental Illness, March 2021, "Mental Health by the Numbers," https://www.nami.org/mhstats.

8. Harold G. Koenig, Dana E. King, and Verna Benner Carson, *Handbook of Religion and Health*, 2nd ed. (Oxford University Press, 2012).

9. Koenig, King, and Carson, *Handbook of Religion and Health*, 2nd ed.; Harold G. Koenig, Michael E. McCullough, and David B. Larson, *Handbook of Religion and Health*, 1st ed. (Oxford University Press, 2001).

10. There are a growing number of resources to address and support the ethical integration of clients' religion and spirituality in mental health care. Some of these are noted under the resources tab on my website, although a few worth elevating here include: Cassandra Vieten and Shelley Scammel, *Spiritual and Religious Competencies in Clinical Practice* (New Harbinger, 2016); Kenneth I. Pargament, *Spiritually Integrated Psychotherapy: Understanding and Addressing the Sacred* (Guilford Press, 2007); Russell Siler Jones, *Spirit in Session: Working with Your Client's Spirituality (and Your Own) in Psychotherapy* (Templeton Press, 2016); and Edward R. Canda, Leola Dyrud Furman, and Hwi-Ja Canda, *Spiritual Diversity in Social Work Practice: The Heart of Helping*, 3rd ed. (Oxford University Press, 2019). Additionally, Dr. Harold Koenig has published a series of six individual books on the intersection of various religions/philosophies entitled [*Buddhism, Catholic Christianity, Hinduism, Islam, Judaism, Protestant Christianity*] *and Mental Health: Beliefs, Research, and Applications.*

11. Laura E. Captari et al., "Integrating Clients' Religion and Spirituality Within Psychotherapy: A Comprehensive Meta-analysis,"

Journal of Clinical Psychology 74, no. 11 (2018): 1938–1951; see also Timothy B. Smith, Jeremy Bartz, and P. Scott Richards, "Outcomes of Religious and Spiritual Adaptations to Psychotherapy: A Meta-analytic Review," *Psychotherapy Research* 17, no. 6 (2007): 643–655.

12. Harold G. Koenig, "Religion, Spirituality, and Health: The Research and Clinical Implications," *International Scholarly Research Network Psychiatry, 2012*, 1–33; Koenig, King, and Carson, *Handbook of Religion and Health*, 2nd ed.; Koenig, McCullough, and Larson, *Handbook of Religion and Health*, 1st ed.

13. In addition to the studies under note 11, which include a variety of treatment modalities, I recommend David H. Rosmarin, *Spirituality, Religion, and Cognitive-Behavioral Therapy: A Guide for Clinicians* (Guildford Press, 2018); Michelle Pearce, *Cognitive Behavioral Therapy for Christians with Depression: A Practical Tool-Based Primer* (Templeton Press, 2016); Harold G. Koenig et al., "Effects of Daily Spiritual Experiences of Religious Versus Conventional Cognitive Behavioral Therapy for Depression," *Journal of Religion and Health* 55, no. 5 (2016): 1763–1777.

14. Philip S. Wang, Patricia A. Berglund, and Ronald C. Kessler, "Patterns and Correlates of Contacting Clergy for Mental Disorders in the United States," *Health Services Research* 38, no. 2 (2003): 647–673.

15. Kevin A. Harris, Brooke E. Randolph, and Timothy D. Gordon, "What Do Clients Want? Assessing Spiritual Needs in Counseling: A Literature Review," *Spirituality in Clinical Practice* 3, no. 4 (2016): 250–275.

16. John Templeton Foundation, "January 2018–December 2019: Fostering Spiritual and Religious Competencies in Mental Health Care (Grant #60971)," https://www.templeton.org/grant/fostering-spiritual-and-religious-competencies-in-mental-health-care. Dr. Kenneth Pargament was the principal investigator for this

grant, and Drs. Michelle Pearce, Cassandra Vieten, and I served as co-investigators, each taking one of three aims of the study. You can learn more about this study at https://sites.baylor.edu/spiritual -competencies-for-mental-health-professionals. You can also learn about our interdisciplinary team's follow-up study with Drs. Joseph Currier, Clay Polson, and Jesse Fox here: John Templeton Foundation, "August 2021–July 2024: Catalyzing a Cultural Shift Toward Integrating Religious and Spiritual Competencies in Mental Health Care Through Training and Systems-Level Change (Grant #62033)," https://www.templeton.org/grant/catalyzing-a-cultural -shift-toward-integrating-religious-and-spiritual-competencies -in-mental-health-care-through-training-and-systems-level -change.

17. Holly K. Oxhandler et al., "The Relevance of Religion/Spirituality to Mental Health: A National Survey of Current Clients' Views," *Social Work* 66, no. 3 (2021): 254–264.

18. Holly K. Oxhandler et al., "Current Mental Health Clients' Attitudes Regarding Religion and Spirituality in Treatment: A National Survey," *Religions* 12, no. 6 (2021): 371.

19. Kenneth I. Pargament, *The Psychology of Religion and Coping: Theory, Research, Practice* (Guilford Press, 1997); see also Kenneth I. Pargament, Margaret Feuille, and Donna Burdzy, "The Brief RCOPE: Current Psychometric Status of a Short Measure of Religious Coping," *Religions* 2 (2011): 51–76.

20. Paul Froese and Christopher Bader, *America's Four Gods: What We Say About God—and What That Says About Us* (Oxford University Press, 2015); see also Association of Religion Data Archives, "The God Test," http://www.thearda.com/whoisyourGod/fourgods.

21. Julie J. Exline et al., "The Religious and Spiritual Struggles Scale: Development and Initial Validation," *Psychology of Religion and Spirituality* 6, no. 3 (2014): 208–222.

22. Tom W. Smith et al., General Social Surveys, 1972–2018, National Opinion Research Center, University of Chicago, 2018, https://gssdataexplorer.norc.org/variables/4714/vshow.

Chapter 3

1. A. K. Krishna Nambiar, *Namaste: Its Philosophy and Significance in Indian Culture* (Spiritual India Publishing, 1979), 20.

2. Gordon W. Allport and J. Michael Ross, "Personal Religious Orientation and Prejudice," *Journal of Personality and Social Psychology* 5 (1967): 432–443, at 434.

3. Allport and Ross, "Personal Religious Orientation," 434.

4. These three points at the beginning of the sentence are based on the Duke University Religion Index's three-item intrinsic religiosity subscale, which is the instrument I've used to measure intrinsic religiosity in my research. Harold G. Koenig and Arndt Büssing, "The Duke University Religion Index (DUREL): A Five-Item Measure for Use in Epidemiological Studies," *Religions* 1, no. 1 (2010): 78–85.

5. Holly K. Oxhandler et al., "The Integration of Clients' Religion/Spirituality in Social Work Practice: A National Survey," *Social Work* 60, no. 3 (2015): 228–237; Holly K. Oxhandler and Danielle E. Parrish, "Integrating Clients' Religion/Spirituality in Clinical Practice: A Comparison Among Social Workers, Psychologists, Counselors, Marriage and Family Therapists, and Nurses," *Journal of Clinical Psychology* 74 (2018): 680–694. We've also seen this pattern among social work educators when it comes to teaching students to integrate clients' spirituality, with intrinsic religiosity the top predictor and training secondary. Holly K. Oxhandler, Edward C. Polson, and Kelsey M. Moffatt, "The Religious/Spiritually Integrated Practice Assessment Scale for Educators: A National Survey of Social Work Faculty," *Journal of Social Work Education* (in press).

6. Oxhandler et al., "The Integration of Clients' Religion/Spirituality in Social Work Practice: A National Survey"; Oxhandler and Parrish, "Integrating Clients' Religion/Spirituality in Clinical Practice: A Comparison Among Social Workers, Psychologists, Counselors, Marriage and Family Therapists, and Nurses."

7. Oxhandler, Polson, and Moffatt, "The Religious/Spiritually Integrated Practice Assessment Scale for Educators: A National Survey of Social Work Faculty"; see also Holly K. Oxhandler and Kenneth I. Pargament, "Measuring Religious and Spiritual Competence Across Helping Professions: Previous Efforts and Future Directions," *Spirituality in Clinical Practice* 5, no. 2 (2018): 120–132; see also Oxhandler and Parrish, "Integrating Clients' Religion/Spirituality in Clinical Practice," and Oxhandler et al., "The Integration of Clients' Religion/Spirituality in Social Work Practice."

8. Holly K. Oxhandler, "Namaste Theory: A Quantitative Grounded Theory on Religion and Spirituality in Mental Health Treatment," *Religions* 8, no. 9 (2017): 168.

9. Holly K. Oxhandler and Traber D. Giardina, "Social Workers' Perceived Barriers to and Sources of Support with Integrating Clients' Religion/Spirituality in Practice," *Social Work* 62, no. 4 (2017): 323–332.

10. Holly K. Oxhandler, Kelsey M. Moffatt, and Traber D. Giardina, "Clinical Helping Professionals' Perceived Support, Barriers, and Training to Integrate Clients' Religion/Spirituality in Practice," *Spirituality in Clinical Practice* 6, no. 4 (2019): 279–291.

11. There are many interpretations of this word, as described under note 11 in the introduction. Again, I've sought to humbly lean on what I've understood of this word from Nambiar's writing. While some see *Namaste* solely as a general greeting, Nambiar both acknowledged the term as a general greeting and was clear about the term being connected to our spirituality.

12. Nambiar, *Namaste.*

13. Nambiar, *Namaste*, 5.

14. Nambiar, *Namaste*, 7.

15. Nambiar, *Namaste*, 15.

16. Nambiar, *Namaste*, 20–21.

17. Oxhandler, "Namaste Theory," 168.

18. Peter C. Hill et al., "Conceptualizing Religion and Spirituality: Points of Commonality, Points of Departure," *Journal for the Theory of Social Behavior* 3, no. 1 (2000): 51–77, at 64. It's worth elevating the last sentence in this quote, which mirrors Nambiar's last sentence in note 16. In both, attention is given to the Sacred/spirit as part of the integration of one's personality.

19. Henri J. M. Nouwen, *Letters to Marc About Jesus: Living a Spiritual Life in a Material World* (Harper & Row, 1988), 69.

Chapter 4

1. Jalāl al-Dīn Rūmī, *The Essential Rumi: New Expanded Edition*, trans. Coleman Barks, (HarperOne, 2004), 20.

2. Henri J. M. Nouwen, *Lifesigns: Intimacy, Fecundity, and Ecstasy in Christian Perspective* (Image Books, 1986), 51.

3. James O. Prochaska and Carlo C. DiClemente, "Stages and Processes of Self-Change of Smoking: Toward an Integrative Model of Change," *Journal of Consulting and Clinical Psychology* 51, no. 3 (1983): 390–395. Note: This was the original study that gave way for the Transtheoretical Model. A number of studies have since been done by the authors examining this model. See James O. Prochaska and Wayne F. Velicer, "The Transtheoretical Model of Health Behavior Change," *American Journal of Health Promotion* 12, no. 1 (1997): 38–48.

4. World Health Organization, "Burn-out: An 'Occupational Phenomenon': International Classification of Diseases," May 28, 2019, https://www.who.int/mental_health/evidence/burn-out/en.

5. Ben Wigert and Sangeeta Agrawal, Gallup, "Employee Burnout, Part I: Five Main Causes," July 12, 2018, https://www.gallup.com /workplace/237059/employee-burnout-part-main-causes.aspx.

6. Massachusetts Medical Society, "A Crisis in Health Care: A Call to Action on Physician Burnout," 2018, https://cdn1.sph.harvard .edu/wp-content/uploads/sites/21/2019/01/PhysicianBurnout Report2018FINAL.pdf.

7. Holly K. Oxhandler, "Advancing the Integration of Religion and Spirituality in Mental Health Care: Measurement and Current Implementation" (data set, 2013).

8. Holly K. Oxhandler, "Integration of Clients' Religion/Spirituality Among Helping Professionals Across Texas" (data set, 2015).

9. Moïra Mikolajczak, James J Gross, and Isabelle Roskam, "Parental Burnout: What Is It, and Why Does It Matter?," *Clinical Psychological Science* 7, no. 6 (2019): 1319–1329.

10. Isabelle Roskam, Maria-Elena Brianda, and Moïra Mikolajczak, "A Step Forward in the Conceptualization and Measurement of Parental Burnout: The Parental Burnout Assessment (PBA)," *Frontiers in Psychology* 9 (2018): 758.

11. Annette K. Griffith, "Parental Burnout and Child Maltreatment During the COVID-19 Pandemic," *Journal of Family Violence* (June 2020), advanced online publication, doi: 10.1007/s10896-020-00172-2; see also Jasmin S. Searcy-Pate and Erlanger A. Turner, "The Impact of COVID-19 on Parental Burnout," *Psychology Today*, February 23, 2021, https://www.psychologytoday.com /us/blog/the-race-good-health/202102/the-impact-covid-19 -parental-burnout.

12. Aisha Harris, "The History of Mister Rogers' Powerful Message," *Slate*, April 16, 2013, https://slate.com/culture/2013/04/look-for-the -helpers-mister-rogers-quote-a-brief-history.html; see also Fred Rogers's reflection of this story in his acceptance speech for the 1997 Emmy Lifetime Achievement Award, https://interviews

.televisionacademy.com/interviews/fred-rogers, chapter 7 of 9 at 6:52.

13.   Charles R. Figley, "Compassion Fatigue as Secondary Traumatic Stress Disorder: An Overview," in *Compassion Fatigue: Coping with Secondary Traumatic Stress Disorder in Those Who Treat the Traumatized*, ed. Charles R. Figley (Brunner-Routledge, 1995), 1–20, at 1.

14.   Trisha Dowling, "Compassion Does Not Fatigue!" *Canadian Veterinary Journal* 59, no. 7 (2018): 749–750; Figley, "Compassion Fatigue," 7.

15.   Rachel S. Rauvola, Dulce M. Vega, and Kristi N. Lavigne, "Compassion Fatigue, Secondary Traumatic Stress, and Vicarious Traumatization: A Qualitative Review and Research Agenda," *Occupational Health Science* 3 (2019): 297–336. With regards to this overall topic of burnout, I also highly recommend the following book: Emily Nagoski and Amelia Nagoski, *Burnout: The Secret to Unlocking the Stress Cycle* (Ballantine Books, 2019).

16.   Katie Baird and Amanda C. Kracen, "Vicarious Traumatization and Secondary Traumatic Stress: A Research Synthesis," *Counselling Psychology Quarterly* 19, no. 2 (2006): 181–188.

17.   Richard Rohr, *Falling Upward: A Spirituality for the Two Halves of Life* (Jossey-Bass, 2011).

Chapter 5

1.   Erin Loechner, *Chasing Slow: Courage to Journey Off the Beaten Path* (Zondervan, 2017), 88.

2.   Holly K. Oxhandler, Sarah C. Narendorf, and Kelsey M. Moffatt, "Religion and Spirituality Among Young Adults with Severe Mental Illness," *Spirituality in Clinical Practice* 5, no. 3 (2018): 188–200.

3.   Holly K. Oxhandler et al., "Integrating Social Workers' Christian Faith in Social Work: A National Survey," *Social Work and Chris-*

tianity 48, no. 1 (2021): 52–74; see also Holly K. Oxhandler, Rick Chamiec-Case, and Terry Wolfer, "A Pilot Study to Develop and Validate the Social Workers' Integration of Their Faith—Christian (SWIF-C) Scale," *Social Work and Christianity* 46, no. 2 (2019): 57–78.

4. Holly K. Oxhandler, James W. Ellor, and Matthew S. Stanford, "Client Attitudes Toward Integrating Religion/Spirituality in Mental Health Treatment: Scale Development and Client Responses," *Social Work* 63, no. 4 (2018): 337–346; see also Matthew S. Stanford, Holly K. Oxhandler, and James W. Ellor, "Assessing the Usefulness of the God Questionnaire," *Psychology of Religion and Spirituality* 13, no. 1 (2021): 46–52.

5. Holly K. Oxhandler and Danielle E. Parrish, "Integrating Clients' Religion/Spirituality in Clinical Practice: A Comparison Among Social Workers, Psychologists, Counselors, Marriage and Family Therapists, and Nurses," *Journal of Clinical Psychology* 74 (2018): 680–694; see also Holly K. Oxhandler, "Revalidating the Religious/ Spiritually Integrated Practice Assessment Scale with Five Helping Professions," *Research on Social Work Practice* 29, no. 2 (2019): 223–233.

6. T. Laine Scales and Helen Harris, Diana R. Garland School of Social Work, "Meet Founding Dean Dr. Diana R. Garland," https:// socialwork.web.baylor.edu/about-us/glance/our-history/meet -founding-dean-dr-diana-r-garland.

7. Shauna Niequist, *Present Over Perfect: Leaving Behind Frantic for a Simpler, More Soulful Way of Living* (Zondervan, 2016); Rachel Macy Stafford, *Hands Free Life: Nine Habits for Overcoming Distraction, Living Better, and Loving More* (Zondervan, 2015); Loechner, *Chasing Slow.*

8. Richard Rohr, "Suffering: Week 1, Transforming Pain," October 17, 2018, https://cac.org/transforming-pain-2018-10-17.

Chapter 6

1. Morgan Harper Nichols, Twitter post, August 23, 2020, https://twitter.com/morganhnichols/status/1297727853627191297. See also Morgan's Instagram account, https://www.instagram.com/morganharpernichols, and her books: *How Far You Have Come: Musings on Beauty and Courage* (Zondervan, 2021) and *All Along You Were Blooming: Thoughts for Boundless Living* (Zondervan, 2020).

2. Encyclopaedia Britannica, https://www.britannica.com/science/Newtons-laws-of-motion.; National Aeronautics and Space Administration Glenn Research Center, "Newton's Laws of Motion," https://www1.grc.nasa.gov/beginners-guide-to-aeronautics/newtons-laws-of-motion.

3. Healthline, "What Is Diaphragmatic Breathing?," September 25, 2018, https://www.healthline.com/health/diaphragmatic-breathing.

4. Simon Sinek, *Start with Why: How Great Leaders Inspire Everyone to Take Action* (Portfolio, 2009).

5. What my doctor provided was an adaptation of integrated behavioral health, which you can learn more about here: https://integrationacademy.ahrq.gov/about/integrated-behavioral-health.

6. Aundi Kolber, *Try Softer: A Fresh Approach to Move Us Out of Anxiety, Stress, and Survival Mode—and into a Life of Connection and Joy* (Tyndale Refresh, 2020).

7. Pete Walker, "The Four Fs: A Trauma Typology in Complex PTSD," http://www.pete-walker.com/fourFs_TraumaTypologyComplexPTSD.htm; see also Pete Walker, "Codependency, Trauma, and the Fawn Response," 2003, http://www.pete-walker.com/codependencyFawnResponse.htm.

8. Kolber, *Try Softer*, 81.

9. Although I wrote this letter in January 2020, shortly before I turned in my manuscript in July 2021, I serendipitously saw that Dr. Hillary

McBride had a similar and stunning letter in an advanced copy of her book, *The Wisdom of Your Body*. When I contacted her about it, she immediately responded to celebrate the connection and shared her 2018 blog post with the same letter: https://hillary lmcbride.com/dear-body-im-sorry-i-love-you. I highly recommend reading her letter and checking out the prompts within her book to help readers write their own letter.

10. Saundra Dalton-Smith, *Sacred Rest: Recover Your Life, Renew Your Energy, Restore Your Sanity* (FaithWords, 2017); see also https://www.restquiz.com to identify which types of rest you need.

11. Adam Alter, *Irresistible: The Rise of Addictive Technology and the Business of Keeping Us Hooked* (Penguin Press, 2017).

12. See the following documentary for more information: Jeff Orlowski, dir., and Larissa Rhodes, prod., *The Social Dilemma*, Netflix Original, 2020.

13. Henry Cloud and John Townsend, *Boundaries: When to Say Yes, How to Say No to Take Control of Your Life* (Zondervan, 1992).

14. Steven C. Hayes, Kirk D. Strosahl, and Kelly G. Wilson, *Acceptance and Commitment Therapy: The Process and Practice of Mindful Change*, 2nd ed. (Guilford Press, 2016).

Chapter 7

1. Henri J. M. Nouwen, *Letters to Marc About Jesus: Living a Spiritual Life in a Material World* (HarperOne, 1988), 69.

2. To learn more about the impact of various types of meditation across religious traditions, see the following: Sabrina Rose, Ethan Zell, and Jason E. Strickhouser, "The Effect of Meditation on Health: A Metasynthesis of Randomized Controlled Trials," *Mindfulness* 11 (2020): 507–516; see also Harold K. Koenig, *Religion and Mental Health: Research and Clinical Applications* (Academic Press, 2018); see also Thomas G. Plante, *Spiritual Practices in Psy-*

chotherapy: Thirteen Tools for Enhancing Psychological Health (American Psychological Association, 2009).

3. Contemplative Outreach, "Centering Prayer: The Guidelines," https://www.contemplativeoutreach.org/centering-prayer-method; see also Cynthia Bourgealt, "Centering Prayer: The Method," 2017, https://cac.org/the-method-2017-02-13.

4. For more on one study's results, see Jesse Fox et al., "Centering Prayer's Effects on Psycho-Spiritual Outcomes: A Pilot Outcome Study," *Mental Health, Religion, and Culture* 19, no. 4 (2016): 379–392.

5. Jon Kabat-Zinn, "Mindfulness-Based Interventions in Context: Past, Present, and Future," *Clinical Psychology: Science and Practice* 10, no. 2 (2003): 144–156; see also Shauna L. Shapiro and Linda E. Carlson, *The Art and Science of Mindfulness: Integrating Mindfulness into Psychology and the Helping Professions* (American Psychological Association, 2009); Qianguo Xiao et al., "The Mindful Self: A Mindfulness-Enlightened Self-View," *Frontiers in Psychology* 8 (2017): 1752; Joey Fung, *Psychology Today*, September 24, 2016, "The Role of Nonjudgment in Mindfulness," https://www.psychologytoday.com/us/blog/mindful-being/201609/the-role-nonjudgment-in-mindfulness. Additionally, the following article offers a fascinating account of one psychologist's experience of meditation within the Soto Zen tradition for nearly five decades: David T. Andersen, "Reflections on 48 Years of Mindfulness Practice," *Journal of Humanistic Psychology* 61, no. 4 (2021): 650–654.

6. Dialectical Behavior Therapy, "Mindfulness: Letting Go of Judgments," 2021, https://dialecticalbehaviortherapy.com/mindfulness/letting-go.

7. I highly recommend following Mt. Irenaeus's Instagram account for regular prayers and reflections from Fr. Dan Riley: https://www

.instagram.com/mtirenaeus. Or visit their website to learn more, https://mountainonline.org.

8. Danielle Rose, "God Is," on *Defining Beauty*, 2001, https://www .youtube.com/watch?v=6w5ecss3keQ.

9. For more information about the Be Still Prayer and other practices, consider Phileena Heuertz, *Mindful Silence: The Heart of Christian Contemplation* (InterVarsity Press, 2018), 28–29.

10. Michael Gungor and Lisa Gungor, "The Great Homesickness," on *One Wild Life*, 2016, https://www.youtube.com/watch?v =sP3rZ90KiV4.

11. To learn more about Lectio Divina, see Faithward, "Lectio Divina: An Ancient Contemplative Spiritual Practice," https://www .faithward.org/lectio-divina-an-ancient-contemplative-spiritual -practice; see also Dan Burke, "Lectio Divina: What It Is and How It Helps Prayer Life," April 21, 2012, https://spiritualdirection.com /2012/04/21/what-is-lectio-divina-and-will-it-help-my-prayer -life-a-guide-to-lectio-divina.

12. Seth Haines, *The Book of Waking Up: Experiencing the Divine Love That Reorders a Life* (Zondervan, 2020), 222.

13. Holly K. Oxhandler, "For Lent, I'm Giving Up Busyness," March 13, 2020, https://hollyoxhandler.com/2020/03/13/for-lent-im-giving -up-busyness-guest-post-for-catching-your-breath.

14. Brené Brown, *The Gifts of Imperfection: Let Go of Who You Think You're Supposed to Be and Embrace Who You Are* (Hazelden, 2010), 70.

15. Richard Rohr, "Suffering: Week 1, Transforming Pain," October 17, 2018, https://cac.org/transforming-pain-2018-10-17; see also Richard Rohr, *Breathing Under Water: Spirituality and the Twelve Steps* (Franciscan Media, 2011).

16. Robert A. Emmons, *Thanks: How Practicing Gratitude Can Make You Happier* (Mariner Books, 2008).

17. Robert A. Emmons, *Gratitude Works! A 21-Day Program for Creating Emotional Prosperity* (Jossey-Bass, 2013).

18. Henri J. M. Nouwen, *The Genesee Diary: Report from a Trappist Monastery* (Penguin Random House, 1976), 77.

Chapter 8

1. rupi kaur, *the sun and her flowers* (Andrews McMeel, 2017), 233.

2. Fred Rogers, "Won't You Be My Neighbor? (1990)," https://misterrogers.org/videos/wont-you-be-my-neighbor.

3. Fred Rogers, "Good Feeling (1986)," https://misterrogers.org/videos/good-feeling.

4. Twitter, @MisterRogersQuotes, August 18, 2019, "I hope that you'll remember / Even when you're feeling blue / That it's you I like, / It's you yourself, / It's you, it's you I like." https://twitter.com/MisterRogersSay/status/1163051020731256832. The lyrics for the whole song can be found at http://www.neighborhoodarchive.com/music/songs/its_you_i_like.html. Based on the content in the video and the episodes listed beneath the lyrics, it appears this clip came from episode 1655: http://www.neighborhoodarchive.com/mrn/episodes/1655/index.html.

5. Sister Mary Sarah Macht, "The Sacred Heart: Burning Furnace of Charity," https://sacredheartmercy.org/sacred-heart-1.

6. Lao Tzu, *Tao Te Ching: A New English Version*, trans. Stephen Mitchell (HarperCollins, 1988).

7. Lao Tzu, *Tao Te Ching*, ch. 25.

8. Henry G. Bohn, *A Hand-book of Proverbs* (1855), 514, https://archive.org/details/ahandbookprover01raygoog/page/n525/mode/2up.

9. Richard Rohr, "Suffering: Week 1, Transforming Pain," October 17, 2018, https://cac.org/transforming-pain-2018-10-17.

10. Ryan Kuja, *From the Inside Out: Reimagining Mission, Recreating the World* (Cascade Books, 2018).

11. Kuja, *From the Inside Out*, 7–8.

12. Thomas Keating, *The Human Condition: Contemplation and Transformation* (Paulist Press, 1999), 13.

13. Henri J. M. Nouwen, "You Are Beloved," in *You Are the Beloved: Daily Meditations for Spiritual Living*, ed. Gabrielle Earnshaw (Convergent, 2017), 6.

14. *Psychology Today*, "Big 5 Personality Traits," https://www.psycho logytoday.com/us/basics/big-5-personality-traits; Myers Briggs Foundation, https://www.myersbriggs.org; Richard Rohr, *The Enneagram: A Christian Perspective* (Crossroad, 1989). See also Jerome Lubbe, *The Brain-Based Enneagram: You Are Not a Number* (2020). Interestingly, Dr. Lubbe's approach suggests that while we most identify with one type, we embody all nine to varying degrees. There are many other authors and speakers on this topic of the Enneagram worth considering if you're interested in learning more.

15. Phileena Heuertz, *Pilgrimage of a Soul: Contemplative Spirituality for the Active Life* (InterVarsity, 2017), 47, 53.

16. You can read more of the story behind the labyrinth I walked and about this practice in general here: https://christthekingpriory.com /sbc-blog/2017/5/15/summer-newsletter. Of this description of the labyrinth, I especially appreciated the following: "The message of the labyrinth is: If we truly seek God we will find God. If, touched and transformed by God's presence, we turn outward, to the people and to the world, we will find God there. 'Seek and you will find,' Jesus says and, 'The Father in heaven [will] give the Holy Spirit to those who ask him' (Luke 11:9, 13)."

17. Heuertz, *Pilgrimage of a Soul*, 135.

18. Richard Rohr, "Dualistic and Nondual Thinking: Contemplative Consciousness," January 30, 2017, https://cac.org/contemplative -consciousness-2017-01-30.

19. Keating, *The Human Condition*, 36.

20. Tara Parker-Pope, "The Science of Helping Out," *New York Times*, April 9, 2020, https://www.nytimes.com/2020/04/09/well/mind /coronavirus-resilience-psychology-anxiety-stress-volunteering .html.

21. Contemplative Outreach, "Welcoming Prayer," https://www .contemplativeoutreach.org/welcoming-prayer-method.

22. Quote by Mary Mrozowski, available at https://www.contemp lativeoutreach.org/download/welcoming-prayer-printable -brochure.

23. Richard Rohr, "The Perennial Tradition: Weekly Summary," August 17, 2019, https://cac.org/the-perennial-tradition-weekly -summary-2019-08-17.

24. The version I have is from a handout that Suzanne and Joe Stabile gave attendees during a talk on their visit to Baylor in February 2017. You may also find a similar version of this prayer at the Richard Rohr note above.

25. Allison Fallon, *The Power of Writing It Down: A Simple Habit to Unlock Your Brain and Reimagine Your Life* (Zondervan, 2020), 23.

26. Jalāl al-Dīn Rūmī, *The Essential Rumi: New Expanded Edition*, trans. Coleman Barks (HarperOne, 2004), 122.

27. Henri J. M. Nouwen, "Stay Awake," in *You Are the Beloved: Daily Meditations for Spiritual Living*, ed. Gabrielle Earnshaw (Convergent, 2017), 124.

Chapter 9

1. M. Scott Peck, *The Road Less Traveled: A New Psychology of Love, Traditional Values, and Spiritual Growth* (Touchstone, 1978), 81.

2. Serenity Prayer, https://www.beliefnet.com/prayers/protestant /addiction/serenity-prayer.aspx.

3. Pope Francis, "Encyclical Letter Laudato Si' of the Holy Father Francis on Care for Our Common Home," May 24, 2015, https://

www.vatican.va/content/francesco/en/encyclicals/documents /papa-francesco_20150524_enciclica-laudato-si.html, Section 233.

4. Robert Vore and Holly K. Oxhandler, "Episode 91: Spiritual Bypassing (feat. Dr. Jesse Fox)," January 27, 2020, *CXMH: Christianity & Mental Health*, https://cxmhpodcast.com/show-notes /2020/01/27/91-spiritual-bypassing; see also Jesse Fox, Craig S. Cashwell, and Gabriela Picciotto, "The Opiate of the Masses: Measuring Spiritual Bypass and Its Relationship to Spirituality, Religion, Mindfulness, Psychological Distress, and Personality," *Spirituality in Clinical Practice* 4, no. 4 (2017): 274–287.

5. James W. Fowler, *Stages of Faith: The Psychology of Human Development and the Quest for Meaning* (HarperOne, 1981), 200.

6. World Curling Federation, "What Is Curling?," https://worldcurling .org/about/curling.

7. My daughter, Callie, gets credit for teaching me this lesson. One day, when she was about five years old, she told me that she couldn't find any clean leggings to wear. I suggested that she wear the clean pair of jeans she had and she immediately responded with, "I don't like wearing jeans because they don't feel good on my body." I knew exactly what she meant. Since then, I've carried her wisdom into deciding each piece of clothing that I wear with a filter of whether it feels kind to my body.

8. Mark McMinn, *The Science of Virtue: Why Positive Psychology Matters to the Church* (Brazos, 2017), 95.

9. McMinn, *The Science of Virtue*, 101.

10. McMinn, *The Science of Virtue*, 112–113.

11. Jalāl al-Dīn Rūmī, *The Essential Rumi: New Expanded Edition*, trans. Coleman Barks (HarperOne, 2004), 36.

12. Interfaith Youth Core, https://ifyc.org; Interfaith Alliance, https:// www.interfaithalliance.org; Parliament of the World's Religions, https://parliamentofreligions.org. See also Eboo Patel, *Interfaith Leadership: A Primer* (Beacon Press, 2016).

Chapter 10

1. Henri J. M. Nouwen, "Love Remembers," in *You Are the Beloved: Daily Meditations for Spiritual Living*, ed. Gabrielle Earnshaw (Convergent, 2017), 338. It's worth explicitly noting the order in which Nouwen emphasizes the actions ("receive love, deepen love, grow in love, and give love"), again nodding to the need to receive love in order to give it.

2. Nadia Bolz-Weber, "Some Modern Beatitudes: A Sermon for All Saints Sunday," November 6, 2014, https://www.patheos.com/blogs/nadiabolzweber/2014/11/some-modern-beatitudes-a-sermon-for-all-saints-sunday.

3. Josh Carney, "The Helpers (A Pastoral Prayer for 3-15-20)," http://ubcwaco.org/blog/2020/3/15/the-helpers-a-pastoral-prayer-for-3-15-20.

4. Sue Monk Kidd, *When the Heart Waits: Spiritual Direction for Life's Sacred Questions* (HarperCollins, 1990), 48.

5. One of our family's favorite books to read that beautifully elevates the uniqueness with which we were each created is Matthew Paul Turner's *When God Made You* (Convergent, 2017).

6. James W. Fowler, *Stages of Faith: The Psychology of Human Development and the Quest for Meaning* (HarperOne, 1981).

7. William Copeland et al., "Cumulative Prevalence of Psychiatric Disorders by Young Adulthood: A Prospective Cohort Analysis from the Great Smoky Mountains Study," *Journal of the American Academy of Child and Adolescent Psychiatry* 50, no. 3 (2011): 252–261; Jonathan D. Schaefer et al., "Enduring Mental Health: Prevalence and Prediction," *Journal of Abnormal Psychology* 126, no. 2 (2017): 212–224.

8. Ruth Haley Barton, *Invitation to Retreat: The Gift and Necessity of Time Away with God* (InterVarsity Press, 2018), 4, 6–7.

9. Barton, *Invitation to Retreat*, 87.

Chapter 11

1. bell hooks, *All About Love: New Visions* (HarperCollins, 2001), 78–79.

2. Baylor University, "Four Pillars That Are Foundational to *Illuminate*," https://illuminate.web.baylor.edu/four-pillars.

3. Baylor University, "Transformational Education," https://illuminate.web.baylor.edu/four-pillars/transformational-education.

4. The topic of valuing transformational education has been woven into my annual tenure materials since my first semester at Baylor. However, it wasn't until my fifth- and sixth-year reviews' tenure letters (written in late 2018 and 2019) that I included the following, echoing the ways the research was changing me: "I have grown in my awareness that we cannot offer transformational education if we are unwilling to be transformed, which has translated into my commitment to growth, humility, learning, serving others, and being transformed—cognitively, emotionally, and spiritually—in order to offer the transformational education Baylor values."

5. A. K. Krishna Nambiar, *Namaste: Its Philosophy and Significance in Indian Culture* (Spiritual India Publishing House, 1979), 5–21.

6. Nambiar, *Namaste*, 20.

7. Seth Haines, *The Book of Waking Up: Experiencing the Divine Love That Reorders a Life* (Zondervan, 2020), 222.

8. Stanford University, Martin Luther King, Jr. Research and Education Institute, "Heschel, Abraham Joshua," https://kinginstitute.stanford.edu/encyclopedia/heschel-abraham-joshua.

9. Henri J. M. Nouwen, "In Service We Encounter God," in *You Are the Beloved: Daily Meditations for Spiritual Living*, ed. Gabrielle Earnshaw (Convergent, 2017), 225.

RESOURCES

The resources offered in this section are simple considerations for you along your own spiritual and mental health journey. Many of these have been helpful for me or are resources that I regularly recommend to others. This section is by no means exhaustive. In fact, I encourage you to find the resources that are most helpful for you as you navigate your sacred journey—you are worth receiving the spiritual and mental health supports you need.

Further, if you are interested in exploring other resources related to the intersection of spirituality and mental health, visit https://hollyoxhandler.com/resources. There you will find additional support links, books, podcasts, research, trainings, and more.

Recommended Mental Health Resources

Crisis Text Line: https://www.crisistextline.org/ or text "HOME" to 741741 (U.S.)

Find a local licensed mental health care provider: https://www.psychologytoday.com

Learn more about Alcoholics Anonymous or find a local group: https://aa.org

Learn more about different types of therapy: https://www.psychologytoday.com/us/types-of-therapy

Substance Abuse and Mental Health Services Administration Helpline: https://www.samhsa.gov/find-help/national-helpline or call 1-800-662-4375

Suicide Prevention Lifeline: https://suicidepreventionlifeline.org or call 1-800-273-8255

Recommended Spiritual Resources

Find a spiritual director: Go to Spiritual Directors International, https://www.sdicompanions.org, or, if you're part of a faith community, talk with your faith leader for suggestions. You can also search for nearby spiritual direction training programs and inquire whether they have a list of current spiritual directors or alumni from their program. You may also choose to do a local search within your area and religious tradition.

Spirituality and Practice website: https://www.spiritualityandpractice.com/

Additional Resources

In addition to the books listed on my website, the following are a handful of my favorites from others who have transparently described their journey at the intersection of spirituality and mental health or have written about this topic from a unique perspective. Some of these stories may be triggering, depending on your personal journey. Due to the sensitive topics within some of these books, please consider reviewing the book's summary, reading reviews of it, or discussing the book with a therapist before reading it.

All Along You Were Blooming: Thoughts for Boundless Living by Morgan Harper Nichols

The Book of Waking Up: Experiencing the Divine Love That Reorders a Life by Seth Haines

The Connections Paradigm: Ancient Jewish Wisdom for Modern Mental Health by Dr. David H. Rosmarin

Glorious Weakness: Discovering God in All We Lack by Alia Joy

I Love Jesus, but I Want to Die: Finding Hope in the Darkness of Depression by Sarah J. Robinson

The Rumi Prescription: How an Ancient Mystic Poet Changed My Modern Manic Life by Melody Moezzi

Sacred Rest: Recover Your Life, Renew Your Energy, Restore Your Sanity by Dr. Saundra Dalton-Smith

Try Softer: A Fresh Approach to Move Us out of Anxiety, Stress, and Survival Mode—and into a Life of Connection and Joy by Aundi Kolber

I also suggest checking out the many books that we have elevated on our podcast, *CXMH* (https://cxmhpodcast.com), which include episodes with each of the authors mentioned above. I cohost this podcast with my friend Robert Vore, and the focus of our conversations is on the intersection of faith and mental health. We bring together faith leaders, mental health professionals, and those with lived experiences at this intersection for honest conversations.

Finally, if you're interested in learning more about autoethnography as a research method, I recommend *Essentials of Autoethnography* by Dr. Christopher N. Poulos.

Additional Training for Mental Health Care Providers

If you're a mental health care provider and looking for additional training on this topic, please see the most recent trainings at https://hollyoxhandler.com/resources.

GRATITUDE

After finishing the edits for this book in August 2021, I curiously circled back to one of its earliest drafts from February 2018 to see how it evolved, mindful of the ways I've changed from writing it. I read about my imposter syndrome, the nudge to write this book eighteen months prior, and second-guessing myself on whether I should even write it. I also read how "the divine spark within is . . . teaching me to get out of its way and let it do its work within me so that it can serve others" and that "my why in life is to serve those who serve others." I read the outline of lies hidden within our culture that claim we need to do, earn, know, perfect, prove, perform, and people-please in order to experience love. And I read about how "we must receive love from some source of Love in order to fuel our ability to express and exchange that love."

It is a gift to see the integrity, the consistent core messaging threaded in the first wobbly self-reflective draft from nearly three-and-a-half years ago show up in the final form of this book. Truthfully, I have been changed by the act of surrendering to each morning's practice of writing as I watched the sunrise while moving through the research, emotions, and experiences to write what needed to come out. The research changed me enough to finally begin writing this book in 2018, but the opportunity to write into and through *The Soul of the Helper* in the years since—and in the midst of so many personal and collective experiences—has both transformed me and left me grateful.

Conducting the research, living into the findings, and writing this book were not done in isolation. There are many whose wisdom, love, time, and attention shaped this book, whom I hope to humbly honor below.

To Susan, Dan, Trish, and the team at Templeton Press, thank you for *immediately* catching the vision of this book and working with me to translate the research and theory alongside the story. I'm grateful for your generous support, grace, enthusiasm, and kindhearted spirits throughout the process.

To my agent, Angela Scheff, I cannot thank you enough for taking a chance on this wobbly academic who hoped to steward an idea from my research into this book. I could not have done this without you. Your friendship, encouragement, and wisdom have all been gifts throughout the journey.

To my editor, Seth Haines, thank you for helping me chisel down this book's excess to reveal its essence. Your keen editorial eye, comments and jokes, and meaningful feedback kept my spirits buoyed through the heavy lift of editing.

My deepest gratitude also extends to the organizations who have supported this research along the way, including the John Templeton Foundation, Baylor University, and the Spencer Foundation. I also want to thank the many scholars whose work I draw upon and weave into this book, and the thousands of research participants over the years for their time and responses. My hope is that, as a researcher, I've stewarded the resources to support the research, previous scholars' work, and participants' responses well.

To my dean, Jon Singletary, thank you for your friendship and mentoring over the years, for the research leave that supported writing this book, and for the ways you empower me to be creative in research. To my colleagues, students, and graduate assistants at

Baylor University's Garland School of Social Work: it is a gift to journey beside you, and I'm grateful for the endless ways I learn from and am inspired by you. I also want to thank my most formative mentors (Danielle Parrish, Ken Pargament, Andy Achenbaum, and Luis Torres) and my research colleagues (Clay Polson, Kelsey Moffatt, Michelle Pearce, Joe Currier, Jesse Fox, Cassi Vieten, and many more) for their wisdom and friendship over the years, and to Rich Furman for his writing encouragement and willingness to point me to autoethnography.

There were also many who read versions of this book—from scrappy early drafts to the final manuscript—and offered invaluable insight for which I'm grateful: Luci, Susan, Amanda, Morgan, Kerri, Jon, Robert, Amber, and Angela. And to Rhianna Griffin, thank you for your friendship and for reading each chapter through the final round of edits.

To friends and loved ones who helped me navigate through these stages over the last several years—including the Reclaim group, our family's life group (Nancy, Charlie, Katie, TJ, Storey, Graham, Paige, Wesley, Alisha, and Tommy), and our neighbors (Rhianna and Chris)—thank you. Your love over the years has shaped me and my family more than you'll ever know. And to my doctor, Bill, who offered that twelve-item prescription—thank you for always caring for me as a whole person.

To Rod, thank you for your presence during each hour of therapy you offered for me to unpack my thoughts, emotions, and experiences. Thank you for helping me discern what's mine to carry or set down, lean into my growth edges, and heal from layers of trauma. This book would not exist without your loving support throughout the whole process. And to Peter and so many therapists mentioned in this book who have held space for my story and process of becoming over the years: thank you.

This book would also not be what it is without the spiritual direction and friendship from Phileena. Thank you for every drop of wisdom, kindness, and love you've offered me throughout this journey. I am also grateful for so many faith leaders who have humbly shaped my faith journey over the years, including Mary Alice, Josh, Brady, Dan, Fr. Dan, Br. Joe, and more. I want to especially thank Josh Carney for offering us *The Helpers (A Pastoral Prayer for 3-15-20)* and for allowing me to share it in this book.

To my dear friend and podcast partner, Robert Vore, thank you for your grounded and loving friendship. You are a gift in my life, and I consider myself among the luckiest to know you and partner with you on CXMH podcast.

To our CXMH guests who have taught and shaped me (many whose words are threaded throughout this book) and to our listeners: thank you. I also want to thank so many friends who have stood at this intersection with me over the years, many whose wisdom also helped me navigate the publishing process: Aundi Kolber, Sarah J. Robinson, Dr. Jonathan Singer, Dr. Altaf Husain, Ryan Kuja, Marlena Graves, Melody Moezzi, Courtney Ellis, and Jeremy Everett.

I'm deeply grateful for the musicians who carried my heart and soul through this writing process. Both volumes of Michael Gungor and Tyler Chester's *On Earth* albums were the daily backdrop as I wrote while watching the sunrise. Others include Dave Matthews Band, Mat Kearney, Rivers & Robots, India.Arie, Ludovico Einaudi, Charlie Cunningham, Gungor, Sleeping at Last, Nichole Nordeman, Jason Mraz, JJ Heller, Andy Grammer, Sara Bareilles, Fleet Foxes, and the Staves. Your music served my soul, offering the soundtrack for these words to dance out of my chest, and carried me when sentences and tears unexpectedly poured out. I'm deeply grateful for your creativity and courage to share your music with us.

To those who offered endorsements for this book, thank you for your generosity, your presence, and your sincere support. Your work inspires me and your words are a gift.

And to you, the reader: I've held you in my heart, mind, soul, and being each day as I sat down to write, and I'm humbly grateful for the ways you've shaped me without even realizing it. Thank you for who you are, for the ways you show up to bring healing and wholeness in our world (including healing your own pain), and for offering your precious time and attention to what I've written for us. I honor the image of God within you and am grateful for your willingness and courage to seek the Sacred within as you serve others.

There are many others who had some direct or indirect influence on this book that would far extend this already long list. I hope you know how grateful I am for the ways you've impacted me and this work.

To my family, those who have seen and loved me for so many years, I love you and am deeply grateful for your presence in my life. Susan and Kelly Case, your unwavering love and sacrificial support throughout the course of my life feels like an extension of God's presence in the world. Mom, thank you for your steady, tender love through many good and tumultuous years, for creating a safe home for me to heal, for consistently believing in me, and for modeling love, integrity, and courage. Dad, thank you for embodying a selfless, fatherly love that valued and empowered me to believe in myself, and for adopting me as your daughter all those years ago. Thank you both for your support of mental health therapy all those years—it set the course for my entire life. To Amanda, Morgan, Richard, and Justin, it is a gift to be your sister and I love you each dearly. Amanda, I'm especially grateful for our journey together and that we've come home to one another. To my in-laws, Naomi and Neil Oxhandler, thank you for your consistent love and encouragement, for happily helping with Callie during those dissertation years, and for all of the ways you unconditionally support our family. To my biological father, I forgive you and wish you well along your journey. And to my extended family, thank you for the times you offered me a safe home when I was young, for the childhood memories that sparkle with love, and for your presence over the years.

To my beloved partner, Cory—your steady, wholehearted, and grounded love all these years is the clearest evidence of God's love in my life. You've believed in me since our first date and continue to believe in me through every season we navigate together. Thank you for seeing and loving me as I am, for cheering me on through my research and through writing this book, and for continually helping me to heal throughout these years. You are the love of my life, and I'm eternally grateful for your steadfast love and presence in our world.

To my darlin' daughter and sweet son, Callie and Oliver, you teach me to see the Sacred within as you fiercely and fearlessly shine your own divine spark. You both love me into being in a way no one ever has or could. As I wrote this book, you'd sneak into my office to snuggle in the early morning hours, draw pictures to cover my office walls, or bring me your "stuffies" to keep me company. This book is for you both, as I pray that you seek the Sacred throughout your precious journey. May you see the divine spark within you as I do and the radiant light it offers our world. I love you both so much and am eternally grateful to be your mom.

Finally, to that divine spark within me and my fellow travelers: you are a never-ending mystery to me. I'm captivated by the ways you lead us home to you and to one another, as I contemplate Ram Dass's wise words, "We're all just walking each other home." You've guided me since I took my first breath and I'm grateful for each unpromised moment I'm given to sense you within myself and others as I seek to serve. Thank you for orchestrating for Jesus of Nazareth to be my guide on how to be human and how to wake up to the Sacred within, while allowing me to humbly learn from other faith traditions along the way. Most importantly, thank you for your whispers of my true identity, that *I am the Beloved*, spoken through Henri Nouwen's words, during my daily surrender in centering prayer, and on that sunny fall afternoon in the earthy center of the labyrinth. Above all, thank you for reminding me, *"I created you and I love you. You don't need to do anything for that love—it's here. I could not love you any more, and I could not love you any less. I love you as you are."* I am humbly and wholeheartedly grateful.

ABOUT THE AUTHOR

Photo credit: Robert Rogers/Baylor University

Holly K. Oxhandler, PhD, LMSW, is an associate professor and associate dean for research and faculty development at Baylor University's Diana R. Garland School of Social Work. For over a decade, Dr. Oxhandler has studied and developed tools to assess mental health care providers' integration of clients' spirituality in treatment, helping professionals' infusion of their own faith in their work, and clients' views toward discussing their spirituality in mental health care.

Dr. Oxhandler has written extensively for top professional journals within social work and psychology, and her research has been featured in the *Washington Post*, *Religion News Service*, and more. She also cohosts the weekly podcast *CXMH: A Podcast on Faith and Mental Health*.

She lives in Waco, Texas, with her husband, Cory, and their two children, Callie and Oliver.

www.hollyoxhandler.com
Facebook.com/HollyOxhandler
Twitter and Instagram: @hollyoxhandler